DISABILITY AWARENESS
IN THE CLASSROOM

ABOUT THE AUTHORS

Lorie Levison was both surprised and honored to find herself writing this book, a project which turned out to be profoundly life-changing. In 1968 she was injured in a car crash and has used a wheelchair ever since, giving her the uniquely personal perspective from which to speak on the subject herein. This book has given her the opportunity to share her insightful observations about living with disability in our society. Believing strongly that most people sincerely wish to be more open and accepting with each other, she has spent time as a disability peer counselor, and each school year presents disability awareness sessions to elementary and secondary students. Her personal experience and research speak for the many others with whom she shares the path of disability. Ms. Levison has a bachelor's degree in English and Secondary Education from Prescott College.

Isabelle St. Onge has been developing the concept of this book for several years, based on her fundamental knowledge of her students as people with value, humor, and ability. Several years ago she began to gather black and white portraits of her students, which eventually became the seeds for *Disability Awareness in the Classroom*. She recognized that the photographs eloquently express the humanity and validity of each student's existence. Throughout her 12 years of teaching students with severe and profound disability, Ms. St. Onge has persisted in creating real-life opportunities of inclusion for her students. Her dedication, along with a rarely-failing ability to laugh at life's surprises, eventually led to the idea of project-based inclusion (Chapter 6), a model which is being presented for the first time in this publication. Mother of three boys, Ms. St. Onge has a masters degree in Special Education from the University of New Mexico.

DISABILITY AWARENESS IN THE CLASSROOM

A Resource Tool for Teachers and Students

By

LORIE LEVISON
ISABELLE St. ONGE

Charles C Thomas
PUBLISHER • LTD.
SPRINGFIELD • ILLINOIS • U.S.A.

Published and Distributed Throughout the World by

CHARLES C THOMAS • PUBLISHER, LTD.
2600 South First Street
Springfield, Illinois 62794-9265

© *1999 by* CHARLES C THOMAS • PUBLISHER, LTD.
ISBN 0-398-06953-0 (spiral) paper

Library of Congress Catalog Card Number: 99-17943

Printed in the United States of America
CR-R-3

Library of Congress Cataloging in Publication Data

Levison, Lorie.
    Disability awareness in the classroom : a resource tool for
teachers and students / by Lorie Levison, Isabelle St. Onge.
        p.   cm.
    Includes bibliographical references (p.) and index.
    ISBN 0-398-06953-0
    1. Inclusive education--United States. 2. Handicapped--Study and
teaching--United States. 3. Handicapped--Education--United States.
I. St. Onge, Isabelle. II. Title.
LC1201.L46 1999
371.9'046--dc21

99 17943
CIP

Dedicated to
Reilly Patrick McCluskey
Maurice Concha
and
their very special parents

ACKNOWLEDGMENTS

This book is a culmination of sorts for both Ms. Levison and Ms. St. Onge, bringing into focus their individual work of many years. The path that brought us to this point was assisted by many individuals, who provided us with their expertise, recommendations, humor and support throughout.

Bill Davis, our primary photographer, has been working with Isabelle for over two years towards the eventual publication of this book. He has photographed throughout northern New Mexico and the Four Corners region for over three decades, and his black and white prints appear in the permanent collections of The Museum of Fine Art, Santa Fe; The Albuquerque Museum of Art; The Harwood Museum, Taos; and Yale University. Bob Blair, elementary school teacher and side-line photographer, was happy to fill in some of the photographic gaps. Ted Schooley, musician and photographer, provided us with four of the student portraits.

Sue Goldberg, high school English teacher, and Kat Duff, author of *The Alchemy of Illness*, were our tirelessly dedicated readers. Chapter by chapter, their encouragement and enthusiasm brought an outside perspective so necessary to the writer who is constantly wondering if what she has written has value or even makes sense. Elizabeth Roth, occupational therapist, helped Isabelle develop project-based inclusion for the past couple of years. She spent hours around the kitchen table with us discussing the do's and don't's of writing about disability, providing skilled editing assistance and information on the special education system and staff.

Drs. Larry Schreiber and Mike Nairn were of great help with Chapter 3: Causes of Disability, educating us with factual information as well as suggestions for organization. Jonathan O'Leary, school district diagnostician, adjusted our information on categories and laws. Author and friend John Nichols (*The Sterile Cuckoo, Milagro Beanfield War*) walked us through the initial stages of contract deciphering. Mike

Levison provided some Internet research for the Recommended Resources section. Our families, children, and friends were continually supportive; special thanks to Jean Kenin, Suzanne Udall, Sally Blair, and Suzanne Frost.

A VERY SPECIAL THANKS

Our deepest appreciation is extended to the students from whom we have learned so much. And to the parents of the students, for their cooperation and courage, and the remarkable dedication they have shown to the rest of the world in caring for children with severe disabilities. They, like us, believe that bringing these children's lives into focus for the education and enlightenment of others gives meaning and purpose to their challenges and dreams.

CONTENTS

TO THE READER

This book started out to be "*not* about inclusion." Yet as it unfolded, it became obvious that there was no way around the issue. Even the title points to inclusion; why else would a book be written about disability in the classroom? The primary intention of this book is to make people feel more comfortable around disability. Whether that is in the classroom or in the supermarket is secondary. However, recent legislature has made it clear that public school teachers will be facing more and more inclusion in general ed classes, as buildings are made accessible and students with severe disabilities are enrolled in school. In response to this situation, there is a need for awareness of unconscious negative attitudes and how to change them, within oneself and in one's students. As attitudes change, so will ideas about inclusion and how to best meet the needs of students with disability.

The domain of public school inclusion policy is broad and wide, full of varying viewpoints and mixed feelings. At one end of the scale is full inclusion, which promotes the special ed student being included full-time in a general education program. The other end is total separation of students with disability for all educational services. The middle roads, and there are many, propose various ways that students with disability be appropriately included in general education programs. Some propose academic inclusion; others support social inclusion. The key word in this discussion seems to be "appropriate," with the central question being, "What actually works best for a particular student with a particular disability?"

Appropriate inclusion settings take into account the individual needs of the students, which vary as widely as the disabilities they live with. Many students with severe conditions have personal needs which are best addressed by qualified personnel in the privacy of a self-contained classroom. Using the toilet, having diapers changed, and maintaining cleanliness and grooming, are activities which are better accomplished in an environment removed from others who might tease or misunderstand. Forcing a child to remain in a setting that is not suitable for these types of personal needs can be an insensitive decision. Another concern is that students who struggle to keep up with social and intellectual peer activity can become overstimulated, tired and depressed. The self-contained classroom offers periods of refuge and rest, where disability is the norm, and where the student is truly without difference, because difference is the rule, not the exception.

Full inclusion in its essence is a worthy goal. It defines a society that accepts and includes people who are different, and values them as individuals. It portrays a school system that expands academic standards to embrace a multitude of skills and various learning styles. It envisions a classroom where every student has a place to learn and grow, receiving the help needed to accomplish a personal, unique potential. Full inclusion points to a future world that supports and furthers local and global unity. Unfortunately, we just aren't at that point in time....yet. Attitudes toward disability are still filled with fear, rejection and discomfort. Attempts at inclusion vary in their success, but all meet with elements of difficulty and resistance. Times are changing, and people are changing. The movement toward inclusion is valid and necessary, and the more carefully the process is planned, the sooner the goal will be reached.

For these reasons, this book proposes a "next step" solution toward the eventual goal of a truly inclusive school system and society. That next step requires the cultivation of sensitivity to the realities of living with disability. Project-based inclusion is the term used to describe a method of bringing together people with and without disability, to learn about each other and dispel misunderstanding and fear, by working jointly on a project. Designing a project for general and special education students provides a perfect opportunity for interaction and communication, allowing the process of acceptance to occur over a period of time. The students get to experience each other, not through textbooks or lectures, but through day-to-day activities with a tangible job to be tackled together. This method promotes authentic acceptance based on firsthand experience. After all, this is how real life unfolds in the "adult world." We work together with all sorts of abilities and personalities, and we learn to accept and know people through the work-place situations. Once the myths and mysteries surrounding a false stereotype are broken down, diversity can be appreciated rather than avoided. And when experience is the teacher, education is at its best, knowledge remains firmly rooted.

The position of this book is basically pro-inclusion, with qualifications. Full inclusion, despite its lofty ideals, can actually be insensitive and damaging to a student with severe limitations and needs. Segregation, on the other hand, has left many people lonely and rejected. Keeping disability hidden is an attitude whose time has passed; it cries out for transformation. Only education and awareness will lead us out of separation and toward inclusion. To achieve this goal, a schoolroom offers the perfect setting for change, and project-based inclusion provides the means to effect that change. The chapters and lesson plans of this book are presented with the belief that many teachers and students throughout the country will benefit from the guidance offered in these pages. Those of us, with and without disability, who have come together to create this book hope the reader will find answers to old questions, and stimulation to ask new questions. On behalf of all students with disability who are committed to attaining a satisfying quality of life, we thank you for taking the time and making an effort to change your little corner of the world.

DISABILITY AWARENESS
IN THE CLASSROOM

Morning Walk

by JAY UDALL

Each morning as I walk to work I pass them:
a young Hispanic man, his body bent
and twisted by some calamity of blood
and bone that has left him to shuffle slow
inches down the sidewalk, his mother
at his side, holding one arm to steady him
and keep him going. She smiles and greets me
as we pass, while her son makes low moans
perhaps only she can comprehend, and only
sometimes. His brown eyes seem locked
inside the stiffness; his head does not turn
to look. He peers out the side, takes in
what he can that way. What does he see?
What does he feel as they make their way
at the incremental pace of love's patience
through hurried streets where fear and anger
often call to each other and answer in kind,
and beauty shimmers in the cottonwood trees
by the river? What does his mother see?
How she must worry about the morning
she won't be there
to hold her son's withered arm.
There is grace in their halting walk,
something to do with how they move
together, the slow, awkward adjustments
of step to step, feet to hard pavement,
finally indefinable.
I cannot completely know
the mystery of their love and suffering.
They do not know that some tortured nights
I have thought of the two of them
walking the streets of morning,
and felt my heart grow calm and still.

Chapter 1

THE REALITIES OF DISABILITY

Call him Tony. He is a student in your middle school. He is good-looking and bright-eyed, blending easily among the crowds of young people streaming through the hallways of the school. He is not known to be a troublemaker; he always has a ready smile for you when you meet. There is nothing in Tony's appearance that would lead you to think he is anything but an average student, traveling the same academic path as his peers.

But Tony is different: his cognitive functioning is impaired. In his own words, "Half my brain doesn't work." This is apparent by Tony's lack of attention, his inability to stay focused, not only on school work but in conversations with friends, or accomplishing simple tasks. He just isn't present half the time.

One day you are in the supermarket, waiting in the checkout line. You notice Tony a few people ahead of you, buying a magazine and a bag of cookies. The cashier tells Tony the amount he owes, $3.16. Tony stares into his handful of change, painfully conscious of the need to quickly figure out which bills or coins to hand over. His lips silently mouth numbers and amounts; his eyes glance to the left and right, and he shifts his weight from foot to foot.

"Come on, kid, quit fooling around and give me the money!" snaps the impatient clerk. "Don't be making a show of this—you're not the only one on line!"

Turning red with embarrassment, Tony dumps the money into the clerk's hand, mumbling, "Here, you can figure it out," and self-consciously shoves his hands deep into his pockets, lifting his shoulders in an obvious attempt to hide his shame.

This story actually happened to Tony. And whether you know it or not, there is a Tony somewhere in your school. He is one of the "invisibly disabled" in our society, who perhaps feels the cruelest edge of public criticism since he has no way of showing people that he is limited in the way he thinks. Tony has been teased and degraded by students and teachers alike throughout his years in school, with very little recourse to let them know why and how he is different. Invisible disabilities are only one of the many disabilities addressed in these pages. However, each person who lives in our society with a disability would have a story like Tony's to share.

This book was conceived on the premise that prejudice against disability exists in our society, and on the belief that prejudice can be eliminated through education. Perhaps prejudice is too strong a word, since it is not a prejudice based on hatred as much as discomfort. It is a subtle fear of that which is different and unfamiliar. Seeing someone with a profound disability, a fleeting thought occurs: "What if that were me?" from which we quickly turn with a shudder. The discomfort is felt as pity, pity for anyone who has to live such a life. More often than not, discomfort results in the avoidance of that which causes it. For example, a man using a wheelchair notices, repeatedly, that people glance at him and then quickly look away. Or the parents of a child who has multiple disability overhear someone at the next table in a restaurant loudly whisper, "You'd think they would keep the boy at home to feed him!" On their way out, that same person tells the parents what saints they are, how special their little boy is.

A Brief History

Historically, people with disability have been kept hidden from the mainstream of society: "out of sight, out of mind." Until the last few decades, many were institutionalized in state-run residential facilities. Amid horrendous conditions, children and adults alike were housed in large, barren wards, living in filth and isolation. Shortage of staffing prevented these residents from receiving adequate stimulation, nurturing, training, hygiene, and sometimes nutrition. The patients were not considered capable of achieving a valid quality of life, and were hardly valued as human beings. But being hidden away, there was little chance for the public to become aware of this degradation. Parents of the children with disability were themselves victims of the shame and stigma attached to their children's conditions, bearing the guilt of putting them into institutions when they were unable to keep them at home.

All this began to change in the early 1970s, when a federal law (Section 504 of The Rehabilitation Act of 1973) was enacted, forbidding discrimination on the basis of disability in all federal buildings and institutions, and all institutions receiving money from the Health, Education and Welfare Department. The law also required the provision of a free and appropriate public education to students with disability, even those who required individually designed instruction. Their education had to be comparable to that offered to students without disability, and would include special accommodations wherever necessary. This was a civil rights law which applied to all programs and activities receiving federal financial assistance. In 1975, the Education for All Handicapped Children Act (PL 94-142) was enacted as an educational law to assure federal funding to aid states in their efforts to provide equal education opportunities for students with disability. These laws initiated the integration of students with disability, who had previously been restricted to institutions or family homes. The introduction of students with specific physical and cognitive needs gradually led to the development of a system that included a complete special education department along with general education. While access to public school was an enormous step towards bringing children with disability out of isolated settings, these students continued to remain, for the most part, in separate classrooms.

This same 1975 legislative act was amended in 1990, and retitled Individuals with Disabilities Education Act (IDEA). The most recent amendment, in 1997, is titled IDEA-B, also known as the Reauthorization of IDEA. Since 1975, the Act and its amendments address the rights of students and parents, and outline the responsibilities of educators, in the following areas:
- The rights of all students with disability to be educated;
- The requirement for all students to receive fair evaluation of their school participation;
- Individualized education plans (IEPs) to determine, provide, and assess appropriate education for the student;
- Inclusion of students when possible and appropriate in general education programs (least restrictive environment);
- The rights of students and parents to protest educators' decisions;
- The authorization of parents (and students when appropriate) to participate in the development of educational plans for the student.

While these laws were making education an accessible right for children with disability, another movement was becoming concerned with general civil rights issues. Some of these activists had grown up with full use of their bodies and minds, and as adults found themselves suddenly disabled, usually as a result of war or automobile injuries. These folks wanted access to a quality of life comparable to what they had known before. They wanted the freedom of being able to go places, do things, communicate with others, and generally live a full and meaningful life. Others who had lived with disability throughout their lives were also feeling the injustice of being denied access to buildings and transportation, of having to do without the everyday opportunities that most citizens took for granted. Many of these individuals were perfectly capable of working, *if* they could get into the workplace. It was becoming clearer that the problem was not the condition of the individual; the problem was the lack of accessibility which actually created a level of "dis-ability." They were able to do the work, but not able to get in the building. This community began to identify and demand their constitutional rights. They were not asking for benefits or charity; they wanted the right to function and live independently, like the rest of the population. In the 1970s and 80s, it was largely this faction that became the radical voice demanding equal access for all.

As a result, the Americans with Disabilities Act (ADA) was enacted in 1990, putting the United States into the forefront of civilized nations providing public access to people with impaired mobility. This law identifies and protects certain rights for people with mobility and sensory impairments. Availability of ramps, wider bathroom doors, computer technology for communication, and assistive devices of all sorts, now make it possible for more and more people of the disability community to get out of the house and into the schools, workplaces, and restaurants of every city and most moderately-sized towns of our country. Although the ADA is now law, the reality of how persons with disability fit into American society is still influenced primarily by the attitudes and stereotypes that are very much ingrained within our culture.

Making it possible for students with severe disability to join their peers in the school buildings was one step; now the educational community is examining the pros and cons of further including students with disability. To understand the full implications of inclusion, when and how it is best applied, begins with the attitudinal acceptance of people with differences into society. Inclusion as an educational concept cannot be addressed objectively until perspectives are free of fear and discomfort.

Educational rights and civil rights go hand in hand. Approaching civil rights through education offers an additional benefit: it provides both the *physical environment* for inclusion of people with disability (within public schools), and also the *learning environment*—a place to instill new values of tolerance and equality. Children with disability of all forms are becoming more and more visible in our schools. And teachers have primary responsibility for shaping their students' perspectives. Students look to teachers for guidance and for answers.

Opening the Door to Change

Many people are completely inexperienced in relating to someone with a severe disability, either physical or cognitive. It naturally feels uncomfortable to be around those who cannot act in the normal range of what is considered "socially acceptable." What if they cannot shake hands, should I pat them on the shoulder? Maybe they walk unsteadily, will they fall? Will I hurt them if I try to help? What if they drool, or I can't understand what they're saying to me? What if I say the wrong thing, something that might offend them or sound patronizing? These natural anxieties, made larger by the silence that surrounds them, are actually quite easy to overcome, with a little guidance and awareness.

Learning occurs when new information can become incorporated with the familiar. If we do not personally know someone who has a disability, as an individual with a need for friendship and fun, who shares our own fear of failure and our desires for a meaningful life, the chances are good that there will be misconceptions which lead to labeling a person with disability as a "type." Stereotyping creates division among groups of people based on class, race, sex, age, ability, hair or clothing style, or any other identifiable feature. Others are judged not on individual merit, but on the traits applied to their larger group. Lack of personal exposure and familiarity leads to attitudes of separation and superiority. When students think it's humorous to hold their wrist in a strongly contracted position and beat it against their chests, putting on a stupid face and drawling, *"Retard!!"* they are revealing their ignorance of people with deformed limbs, who are not necessarily delayed or retarded. They are also stereotyping disability as a highly offensive and degraded condition.

The key to transforming prejudice is information, which has been, at best, scarce. We need ways to come to know each other, in a safe and structured environment. Teachers and students together need to be able to look inquisitively at the differences in others, to identify the similarities, to ask questions and formulate answers and opinions. Together, we need to see people as people, not as the bodies they inhabit.

Having a student with disability in the class is probably the best teaching tool available, given a sensitive teacher who can identify subtle levels of prejudice in students' behaviors. Personal experience with an individual with severe disability quickly informs us of the simple humanity within the abnormal physiology. Some readers may have had this type of experience, others have not. Within or without the included classroom, there are many opportunities to learn acceptance of diversity in our society. This book helps prepare teachers, and subsequently their students, to welcome into their classrooms children and young people who look, act, think and speak differently than most others.

About Disability Awareness in the Classroom

As a result of the Reauthorization of IDEA-B, schools will be experiencing an increasingly diverse population of learners within the public schools. Teachers need specialized preparation to successfully incorporate students who have regularly been kept separate. The preparation lies in the development of acceptance of diversity, and an appreciation of the value of the individual, regardless of physical or cognitive competence.

Given the existence of prejudice, how will integration take place? The classroom teacher holds a primary responsibility for finding ways to introduce his or her students to the actualities of disability. This challenge in itself is formidable, since repeated studies reveal a notable resistance among teachers to inclusion of students with disability. The reasons for this aversion point to (1) a lack of familiarity on a personal level with someone with a disability, (2) a lack of professional training and preparation in teaching methods, and (3) unsuccessful experience with past inclusion attempts. *Disability Awareness in the Classroom* addresses the first two of these concerns.

The purpose of this book is to reduce the discomfort and alienation of teachers and students regarding people with disability, through written and photographic materials. The intended goal of the book is to raise the level of awareness around what causes disability and the potential quality of life for those with varying abilities. It aims to dispel misconceptions that contribute to stereotyping, and in general to blur the divisions between two segments of our society: those with disability and those without. After all, any one of us could cross that line in a moment, and find ourselves living with disability for the rest of our lives.

As discomfort subsides, new opportunities automatically emerge for support, communication, and friendship. Informed understanding results in more frequent and more meaningful interaction among differently-abled students. A change of attitude leads naturally towards a greater willingness to explore inclusion at all levels of education. Teachers become more open to presenting new approaches, and students become more open to experimenting with new situations.

The text is designed to guide teachers as they present the topic of disability awareness to their students. Since discomfort with disability is an attitude that exists within the very fabric of societal consciousness, everyone needs more information and exposure to begin, and continue, the process of true inclusion. Even when a class has had included students in the past, a presentation on acceptance of differences is an invaluable topic, and will benefit students not only in the school environment, but also in their personal lives.

How to Use Disability Awareness in the Classroom

Disability Awareness in the Classroom is formatted as a teacher's guide, and also as a resource tool for classroom curriculum. The structure is straightforward and simple to use. The chapters can be used separately, or consecutively to form a longer teaching unit. Chapters 1 and 6 (The Realities of Disability and Project-Based Inclusion, respectively) are specifically teacher chapters, and are limited to chapter text only. All other chapters include curriculum sections. The chapters are structured as follows:

• Chapter Text: discussion of a specific topic to help students and teachers understand the realities of life for those with disability, or work together in groups.

• Myths and Misconceptions: common misunderstandings about disability.

• Aware of Our Words and Actions: examples of appropriate and inappropriate ways of communicating with or about those with disability.

• Ideas for Discussion: recommendations for classroom discussion of ideas presented in the chapter text.

• Lesson Plans: games, assignments, and classroom/community projects, by grade level.

• Student Biographies: each chapter presents photographs and a detailed biography on one student with disability.

An integral feature of this book is the separate photo cards, which are also reprinted in full in the Student Biography sections of the text. These cards are provided for a very specific purpose: to be stared at! The photographs give readers the opportunity to look at the "differentness" of others without inhibition, and without hurting anyone's feelings. Children are usually taught that correct manners include not staring in public. However, there is an innate need to look at someone whose body moves and rests in rare and sometimes inexplicable ways. It's natural to want to see, and understand, what the differences are. Careful examination of the photos will also generate a level of intimacy, as readers come to know the young people portrayed, their families, their lives, and their dreams.

The seven sets of photo cards show compelling pictures of students with severe and profound disabilities which capture the students in a variety of situations. The information on the back of the photo cards (also reprinted in the Student Biography sections) gives the young person's biography: how the disability came about, age, inabilities and abilities, challenges, and school and family life. There are also explanations of what the student is doing in each photo, to stimulate awareness of what it might be like for someone with that particular disability. Reflective questions guide students towards "walking in another's shoes." We recommend allowing students to spend as much time as they wish, passing the photos and looking deeply at them. The photos are intended to inspire self-exploring and thought-provoking discussions.

Note to Teachers: the authors strongly recommend that you laminate the photo cards before using them, to protect them from the normal wear and tear of student handling. They are printed on a heavy paper, but are not intended for prolonged use without a plastic covering. Additional card sets are available from the publisher, should the original set become unusable.

At the end of the book, there is an appendix of Recommended Resources and additional information for those interested in developing the topic further.

A Challenge for All

In order to effectively teach appreciation of diversity, each teacher must claim the motto, "Let it begin with me." This book is offered to all educators who believe every individual is valuable in his or her own right, from the high-achieving college-bound student to the totally dependent child who relies on others for every aspect of care and survival. The first may achieve prestigious awards or fame and fortune. But the second—and let us not limit the value of every life—may achieve the humble honor of teaching compassion and generosity in a fast-paced, self-oriented society.

While we call these children "special" they are not greater than the rest of us; more importantly, neither are they less. They bring the world a gift of reflection and challenge: will we see in them our own needs and challenges, coming to learn that we are all in this life together? Or will we continue to separate those who are different, denying the fragile humanity that lies at the core of our fears?

We hope you will come to know and appreciate the children portrayed in these pages. There are many more like them in your own school district. Some of them are still separate and isolated, waiting for the time when they will be included and appreciated. We guarantee that your life will be richer for reaching out to them, learning to recognize the precious gift of "any-ability."

Student Biography: Raymond

1.1: Raymond

Raymond is a young man who was born with a rare genetic disorder. Genetic means it was passed to him from one of his parents, who carried it in their genes without having it themselves. The nervous system in Raymond's body is slowly degenerating; he gets weaker and less mentally aware as he gets older. He has an uncle and younger cousin with the same disability.

Figure 1.1 Raymond (photo by Ted Schooley).

Raymond is tender and caring, often opening his arms to ask for a hug. He has a childlike sense of humor, finding it very funny if someone farts or burps or trips. His laughter at silly things makes everyone laugh. He is also very sensitive to other people's moods, and makes an effort to comfort someone who is sad.

After graduating, Raymond was hoping to attend the Association for Retarded Citizens, which is a program where people with disability can go during the day for projects, activities, and social time. Unfortunately, his family cannot afford to send him, and there is no grant money available from the government. So Raymond spends his days at home, with very little to do but watch television. His mother doesn't have a car, so he can't get out much. He does have a sunny porch he likes to sit on, and a large family of cousins, aunts and uncles who visit him often. This is when he's happiest—in the midst of people he loves.

Questions:

1. Do you think the government should provide money to make sure people like Raymond get to be in a program after they graduate? Explain your answer.

2. Do you think those of us who do not have a disability need to help support people who do?

3. How would you feel if you couldn't get out of your house because of a disability?

1.2: Alone in the Hall

While all the students are in class and the long school hallways are empty, here comes Raymond inching his way along in the wheelchair. It takes him about twenty minutes to come down the hall in the picture, and it's hard work. It's actually part of his school program to push the wheelchair, keeping his arm muscles strong and stimulating his breathing. Every day his assignment was to go from his class at one end of the hall to the Home Economics room at the other end, where he could pick out a magazine from a large pile. He can't read the stories or advertisements, but he enjoys looking at the pictures. Raymond used to read to his mom when he was in third grade, but over time he's lost that ability. He still reads the days of the week.

For five years of high school, Raymond went down that same hall every day. On his very last day of school, just before graduation, he turned with his wheelchair left instead of right, and went down the wrong hall—one with a long ramp. His wheelchair got out of control and crashed. Raymond was knocked unconscious and broke a tooth. He was found quickly and taken to the hospital.

Questions:

1. Why do you think Raymond turned the wrong way on his very last day?

2. What do you think Raymond's feelings are about doing his "schoolwork" alone in the hall?

3. If someone in your family used a wheelchair, what changes would have to be made in your home?

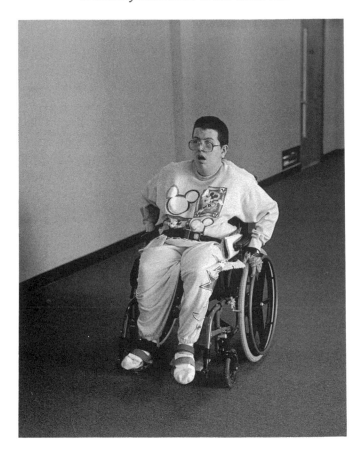

Figure 1.2 Alone in the Hall (photo by Bill Davis).

1.3: The Hoyer Lift

Raymond, as you can see, is a big guy. Raymond's disability causes him to become heavy, even though he has very little use of his muscles. He's not a big eater, but continues to gain weight. One of the problems of being heavy is that it's hard for others to lift him, and so the physical therapists use a device called a Hoyer Lift. Raymond wears a canvas sling under him as he sits in the wheelchair. You can see it in some of the pictures. When it's time to move him, the sling is attached to the Hoyer Lift and cranked up until he is lifted out of the chair. The therapists usually count, "1 - 2 - 3" before lifting him, so he knows when its coming. Then, with Raymond swinging, they roll the Hoyer over to the mat table and lower him, where they will exercise his arms and legs.

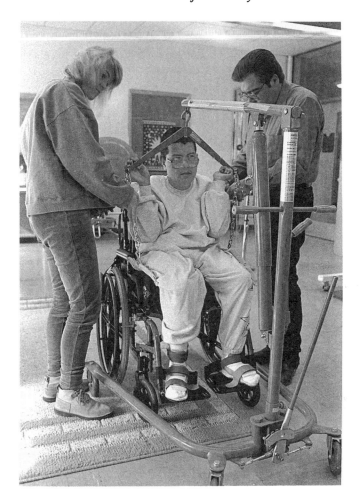

Figure 1.3 The Hoyer Lift (photo by Bill Davis).

He doesn't look very happy in the swing, but Raymond often has that sort of look, even when he's just looking around. He really doesn't mind going in the lift, and he enjoys working on the mat table. It's a break from being in the wheelchair, and it feels good having his body stretched and exercised.

Hoyer Lifts are used in hospitals and swimming pools, to lift and move people who cannot move themselves. Without this kind of equipment, it would take several strong people to move Raymond.

Questions:

1. Raymond doesn't have a Hoyer Lift at home. What other choices does he have for going out or getting around?

2. If Raymond is gradually losing all his abilities, do you think it's a blessing that he's also losing his mental awareness? Do you think it would be better to stay mentally aware even when you lose the physical part?

1.4: Basketball

People with disabilities often enjoy sports, even if they can't play like others. Raymond uses a special basketball hoop that's hardly higher than his head. Because of his body's weakness, it takes a lot of Raymond's strength and energy to throw the ball, even though the basket is so close. But when he makes a basket, he's as proud and happy as a basketball team player who shoots all the way across the court. The other part about scoring that he loves is hearing people clap or cheer for him. Several years ago, Raymond used to be able to make four baskets in a row. As his disability progresses, he's no longer as strong, and now he misses more baskets than he scores. He tires easily, and can't make his body do what he wants it to.

Raymond's weakness has made pushing the wheelchair more and more difficult for him. Sometimes when the school hall is full of students, Raymond will reach his hand out and say one of his few words, "Help!" Usually the student will push him to his classroom. He comes in smiling because he knows he outwitted the physical therapist, who wants him to push himself. Sometimes students don't stop to help Raymond, because they're afraid of how different he is, and uncomfortable with the wheelchair. They pretend not to hear him, and look the other way.

Questions:

1. What if Raymond asked you for a push in the hall? Would you be uncomfortable?

2. Have you ever felt tired and still wanted to do things? How would it be to feel like that all the time? Would you just want to give up?

3. Why do you think some people are afraid of wheelchairs?

Figure 1.4 Basketball (photo by Bill Davis).

1.5: Stacking Cones

Raymond has maintained some very basic skills, like simple hand coordination, stacking cones and sorting. Sorting is when you separate things by size or shape or color. Raymond practices these elementary skills at school. He also sits in on some general education classes, mostly just watching and listening. If something funny or silly happens, he'll laugh. But he doesn't fully understand what's going on around him. If someone got angry and yelled, Raymond might get upset but he wouldn't understand why the person was angry.

He has to wear a diaper now because he's no longer able to tell someone when he needs to use the toilet. Although he can't remember what day it is, he has an incredible memory when it comes to people he's met, remembering someone's name even after not seeing the person for years. His speech is very slow, and sometimes difficult to understand. Raymond makes sentences with two or three words.

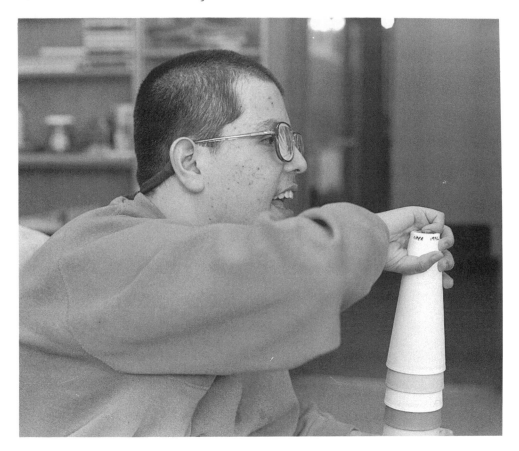

Figure 1.5 Stacking Cones (photo by Bill Davis).

It's hard to know Raymond's feelings about having a disability and growing weaker. Sometimes he gets frustrated, but not very often. He doesn't spend much time complaining, which may surprise you. He continues to enjoy all the little pleasures of his days: someone to hug, sitting in the sun, or a magazine picture of a pretty girl.

Questions:

1. If Raymond is not aware if people make fun of him, does that make it okay?

2. Can you explain how low mental functioning makes people less bored, impatient, or dissatisfied?

3. At what age do you think children begin understanding why someone is angry?

Chapter 2

PREVAILING ATTITUDES

Many people believe that the time has come for disability to lose some of its stigma in our society. The long history of secrecy and shame for families and individuals dealing with disability is slowly coming to an end, as can be witnessed in legislative changes enacted in the past two decades. The public schools have become one of the foremost avenues for change, as more and more students with severe and profound disability are finding their way into classrooms, in both special and general education departments.

A sincere desire to change is also being exhibited these days. People seem to be ready to explore their own hearts and minds, to reduce some of the resistance around connecting with someone with a disability. Many express both desire and relief to learn about accepting and communicating with others who are different physically and cognitively. People are tired of feeling separated by feelings of fear, discomfort, pity, shame, and resentment, which arise naturally within a society that has, for the most part, gone uneducated about disability issues and facts. Unhelpful attitudes are carried by both those with disability and those without. No one side is to blame; all must work together to create a new way. These attitudes are learned unconsciously; they can be unlearned with just a little effort and awareness.

The intention of this chapter is to examine and discuss the more common attitudes found in response to disability. The attitudes listed within this chapter are indeed prevalent, and usually harmful to everyone involved. Identifying one's own attitudes is the surest way to begin changing them. And as attitudes change, so does perspective. You will see people differently; you will see them as less different! As your point of view changes, so will the opportunities that seem to arise naturally: meeting more people with disability, or finding yourself more comfortable in what used to be awkward situations. It takes an effort to change, and change is sometimes hard. But there is magic in the outcome, when it creates more freedom, more comfort, and more humanity.

A Personal Account

I was paralyzed as a young man in a car wreck. Suddenly, I found myself living in a wheelchair, a very different type of experience. My self image changed radically, and I had to face my own feelings as well as the responses of people around me when I would go out in public. I was ashamed, angry, scared, confused, and fiercely determined. The other people seemed to be embarrassed, sorry, and very uncomfortable. Sometimes I felt like it was up to me to make them feel better about my problem.

For several years I wouldn't let anyone push the chair for me, even on a steep hill. That meant that whoever was with me had to walk at a snail's pace to allow me to huff and puff up the hill. I just couldn't stand the thought of being dependent. I didn't want to accept the image of myself as crippled and helpless, just an object of other people's pity. But it felt like that's what the wheelchair automatically turned me into.

After a few years, I noticed that whenever I went past a large window or mirror, I wouldn't look at myself. And also, when I saw other people in wheelchairs, I would look away, not wanting to see them or to have them see me. I didn't want to admit that I looked like them, or that I fell into their category. I didn't want to attract that kind of attention for being different. The actual sight of myself or other disabled people threatened my denial. I was trying to pretend that I was just like everyone else, but sitting down.

So.....to deal with the situation, I went out and bought a full-length mirror and hung it where I had to look at myself every time I went into the bedroom. It helped me to accept myself, as I really am, to look openly at myself and not be afraid of other people's covert glances, or rude stares. Then I began to look at other guys in wheelchairs, because I had lost some of my fear. I was surprised to see that many of them were avoiding looking at me! Sometimes I couldn't get eye contact even if I tried. Now I go out of my way to wave or say hello. If the person in the chair is not mentally aware or able to talk, I connect with whoever is helping them. I want to acknowledge our sameness, because we both face challenges that are unique and difficult.

What I learned from these experiences is that a lot of the people around me fear my disability. It's not ME they fear, but whatever they are seeing with their own eyes. And I carried that same fear in me. I wanted to escape being looked at in a way that judged me as inferior or pitiful. I tried to fool myself, but it didn't work. I had to change my own attitude if I had any hope of others changing theirs. I had to admit that I was very uncomfortable around disabled people, and didn't want to be identified with them. And I had to admit that I was indeed a member of that group, whether I liked it or not.

There are times when I know that people are uncomfortable around me, and they don't know how to act, or what to say. They usually treat my disability as if it's something sad and tragic, and out of politeness they avoid any mention of it. The truth is, being in a wheelchair does make me different in ways, and makes my life different in ways. But it doesn't make ME different, as a person, inside.

This story gives a unique insight into the experience of a wheelchair user. The writer lives with a visible disability, and communicates clearly not only how others react to him, but also his own inner fear and prejudice. It makes sense that he initially wanted to avoid people in wheelchairs, even though he was in the same situation, because he saw disability as a shameful condition. His story illustrates how attitudes lie deep and unconscious within people until an event or situation brings them to the surface. Once aware of those attitudes, we have the choice to change, as he did by buying the mirror and learning to say hello to others.

Speaking Up

Attitudes can be subtly hidden within a society's value system, so ingrained that individual members of the society are not even aware of their own perspectives. When everyone shares the same basic belief, it remains unchallenged, without discussion. It never comes up for examination, until the ones who are being oppressed by the attitude decide it is time for new information. Two recent examples of this type of reaction are the African-American civil rights movement of the 1960s, and the women's liberation movement of the 1970s. When a segment of society becomes aware of its oppression, it begins to "move" things along. These movements all proclaim the same message: "According to our country's constitution, we are created equal, and we deserve to be treated with equality, dignity, and respect, and to have equal opportunities based on our abilities, not the color, gender or condition of our bodies."

The voice of the disability community has been persistent and is gaining confidence. The members of this community are wide-ranging, as disability affects people regardless of age, race, gender, or socioeconomic status. Many very effective changes have been achieved, making it possible for people with all sorts of limitations to live fuller, more rewarding lives. Educational legislation has guaranteed children with disability the right to receive a free and appropriate education; the Americans with Disabilities Act initiated specific requirements for physical access standards nationwide. These laws set new rules externally, but only attitudes will enforce whether people are treated with the dignity and respect due to every citizen of this country.

The Root of Prejudice

Throughout contemporary European history, disability has been hidden away and shrouded in secrecy. After the development of asylums around the 18th century, people with disability were kept in institutions if not at home. They were rarely taken out in public, partly because it was considered unacceptable in society, and partly because there were very few accessible places to go. As a result of such lack of exposure in everyday public activities, disability became associated with hospitals and institutions. Seeing an individual with a severe disability was a rarity in public, and would naturally attract attention.

Fear and rejection of disability are reinforced by society's preference, almost worship, of healthy, youthful bodies. The accepted standard for "beauty" is a narrow one, as demonstrated by movie stars and magazine models. It would be very unusual to see an overweight actor in a serious, romantic role, or an actress with thick glasses playing a sexy part. And yet these situations are daily realities in life. Rarely is a person with disability seen portrayed anywhere in the media. Physical perfection, mental acuity, and verbal proficiency are idolized, while physical and mental impairment or disfigurement are shunned. This situation also affects many others who, although free of disability, still cannot hope to compete with such an impossible standard. So many people feel inferior in some area of existence: too old, too young, too fat, not smart enough, not quick enough, not funny enough.... on and on. These feelings impart a mild experience of disability, with a gut-level reaction of hiding the deficiency from others.

Having a history of hiding our community members with disability, and a current infatuation with beautiful bodies, it is understandable that there is confusion about disability. The exposure and education necessary to dispel fears has been lacking. At least some of those fears have been learned unconsciously through family and societal values. The unconscious values, and the feelings that underlie them, will not normally surface on their own, unless there is a stimulus, for example, coming into contact with a person with disability. Those who have had the opportunity to know intimately a family member or close friend with disability know that values change drastically as a result.

Changing Attitudes through Awareness

Feeling uncomfortable around someone with disability is not a personal or individual shortcoming. It is nothing to be ashamed of; actually, it is normal and natural for anyone growing up in this country. It is an attitude that everyone shares, to a greater or lesser degree. Unless this type of attitude is admitted and made conscious, it can never change. If people maintain they are free of prejudice, they will never see their own blind spots that need removing. Knowing that the attitudes exist throughout society makes it easier, and more essential, to look at the situation and the part each person plays in it.

The first thing to consider is that no oppression is one-sided. Oppression consists of two sides both believing the same thing. In the case of disability, an able-bodied person often feels superior and more capable, which leads to feelings of pity, guilt, obligation, and even revulsion. In response, the person with disability feels inferior, lacking, and oddly different, which causes shame, anger, resentment, and blame. A cycle of victimization is created, where one side feels somehow responsible and the other feels like the loser. The "underdog" points to the oppressor as the one who should change. "They should stop treating us like that." However, this approach only reinforces the feelings of guilt in the unintentional oppressor, backfiring into resentment. "It's not my fault that I have what you want."

The following scene illustrates the shared responsibility in this situation. Imagine a young man with moderate cerebral palsy going to the grocery store. He cannot walk well, his arms and legs make wide, lopsided movements, jerky and unbalanced. His speaking is almost impossible to understand. However, he is perfectly capable of getting down the aisles in his own wild way, gathering his items into a basket, and paying the cashier. Of course, he attracts attention. Other people are uncertain how to act around him. They look away, pretending not to notice his very awkward gait. They avoid talking with him because they probably will not understand him. They fear he might fall, and they will have to be the ones to help him; they don't know how, and they fear they might hurt him. All in all, their reactions communicate fear and avoidance. Meanwhile, the young man is not mentally impaired. Acutely aware of their reactions, he feels belittled and ashamed of his uncontrollable movements. He doesn't dare try to talk to others, because he knows from experience how painful it is when they can't understand his words. He avoids looking at them, withdrawing into himself. Each "side" avoids the other out of fear, shame, discomfort, and uncertainty.

What is needed is a new perspective that transcends inferior/superior notions, and moves towards the concept of accepting and appreciating differences within a wider range of values. Meeting that young man on a personal basis, learning how to understand his speech, and get used to his crooked way of walking, might lead to a new friendship, where he could be appreciated for his thoughts, his sense of humor, his caring, maybe even his excellent music collection! And when one barrier is taken down, with one person, then each new person, regardless of differences and peculiarities, is less frightening, less strange.

Disability Role Models

Disability role models are few and far between. Ask a class of school children what famous disabled people they know. They will probably answer: Helen Keller. Some may know that Christopher Reeves, the movie star who played Superman in the 1978 movie version, became paralyzed from a neck injury. High school science students may be familiar with the writings of Stephen Hawking, a physicist with a degenerative nerve condition known as Lou Gehrig's disease.

In current times, role models are established primarily through media. The media—magazine and newspaper advertisements, television shows, news stories, movies—has infinite power to influence attitudes by showing people with disability as models. Imagine if every time you watched television, there was an advertisement depicting a person with disability, even if that person was just in the background passing by. Picture magazine ads portraying a loving couple, one of whom is in a wheelchair, or a mother feeding her child a bowl of name-brand cereal, where the child happens to have Down's Syndrome.

In response to heavy lobbying by disability advocacy groups in the late 1980s, McDonald's became one of the first corporations to agree to include obvious disabilities in a percentage of their advertising. Other leading brands have followed the lead in subsequent years, but the results appear minimal, and usually shy away from all but the most "inoffensive" disabilities. While advertising has progressed to include people of many nationalities and races, disability remains disproportionately lacking in television, magazines, and movies. An interesting example of the media playing down disability concerns one of our country's past presidents. Franklin D. Roosevelt had polio and used a wheelchair, but was politically careful not to be photographed in his chair. It's surprising how few people in our country even realized that their president had a disability. Without media representation, we lack the opportunities to associate *disability* with *ability*.

Role models are also formed through the people we meet in our lives. According to statistics, about one out of eight people has physical or cognitive disability. Many of these individuals are still staying at home, avoiding the pressures and prejudice of public exposure. Think of how different attitudes would be if throughout towns and cities, in movie theaters, grocery stores, gas stations, or businesses, every eighth person was in a wheelchair or using crutches, was blind, wearing a hearing aid, missing a limb, or using sign language. Disability would become a common sight rather than a rare occurrence to which many well-intentioned people just do not know how to respond.

Visible role models are important for two reasons: (1) to encourage those with disability, and (2) to desensitize those without. People with disability need to see themselves reflected in a positive way to the general public, in order to develop a sense of value and self-recognition. The audience needs to see disability presented in its full scope of reality, from the inspiring challenges and remarkable accomplishments to the disappointments and loneliness of those individuals. When that happens, people on both sides of this apparent division can gain a new understanding of what it means to have a disability.

Common Feelings about Disability

No one should expect to be exempt from having uncomfortable feelings about disability, nor should there be any guilt surrounding those feelings. Understanding what the feelings are, where they come from, and then being presented with some alternative ideas, will help dispel a good deal of discomfort in interactions with people with disability. Some readers will have extensive experience with disability, either through family members, friends, students, or themselves. While you may find that your own feelings have changed significantly as a result of familiarity, you will probably be aware of many of these feelings within the general fabric of society.

Fear

Fear is one of the most prevalent feelings behind society's attitude toward disability. Why is that? Perhaps we are afraid of being in that situation ourselves, which looks like too much suffering, pain and isolation. The person with the disability is like a mirror, reflecting an image of ourselves in that position. It looks frightening, horrible, a life of giving up so many activities and one's independence. Fearful reactions stem from a subconscious desire to avoid thinking about such a possibility. This reaction is natural and actually healthy, the response of a vital organism to preserve life and health for self and family. But taken to an extreme, this impulse is more like sticking heads in the sand, refusing to consider the potentially difficult paths of life.

With such an extensive history of isolation, disability has become associated with lack of friends, lack of enjoyment, lack of meaningful employment or entertainment. The fear of being alone and/or incapable runs very deep for most citizens of the United States, a country built on independence, freedom, and the pursuit of happiness. This same fear is evident in treatment of the elderly, who are similarly seen as having less value because of dependency.

Some people fear that involvement with a person with disability will lead to overwhelming obligation and responsibility. Seeing people with disability as needy or helpless creates a doer/giver role for the one without disability. It creates a fear of being asked to give more, or do more, than what is comfortable. One might also fear that a disability is contagious, and believe that distance is necessary for safety reasons. Both of these fears are products of unrealistic thinking and attitudes. However, if they are not challenged, they continue to reinforce the internal barriers of fear.

A more balanced view realizes that disability can befall anyone at any moment, and if that happens, there is usually a way to cope and live with it. Unconscious fear focuses only on the loss, rather than the true wholeness of the person with disability. Every person is a whole person, even if there are things they can't do. No matter how disabled the body or mind, there is a person "inside" that is vital and human and vulnerable. Fear makes it difficult to see the person that exists beyond the disability. This is a crucial distinction to make, its importance underlined by the movement to use "people first" language. People first language says "people with disability" rather than "disabled people," in order to emphasize that they are people first, and the disability comes second.

Fear also exists within the people who have disability. Their fears are the other side of the same coin. For example, a person with disability might fear going into public places, because of the negative response received from strangers. Or they might be overly independent in order to compensate for the fear of being helpless. Many people with disability fear they will be rejected because of the disability, and in fact they often live with daily experiences of rejection, ranging from mild to extreme. They learn to see themselves the way others see them, and identify with those same fears and attitudes.

Discomfort

Discomfort is not actually an emotional feeling, but is an experience caused by unpleasant feelings or emotions. However, it is the way most people feel when they are around someone with a disability, if they have not had prior education or exposure. The quickest relief of this discomfort is found by removing the stimulus: out of sight, out of mind. Therefore, avoidance becomes a rather successful method for maintaining one's comfort level. For public school teachers, avoidance is no longer a choice. Learning how to act toward someone, speak with someone, and look at someone who has a disability is the only effective cure for discomfort. When what is appropriate is clearly defined, it's easier to relax with ourselves and others. Fortunately, discomfort is not a deep-rooted prejudice, and most people appreciate having this feeling relieved, allowing a freedom of interaction with more individuals in a more relaxed manner.

Pity

People often ask, "Should I feel sorry for someone who has a disability?" It's natural to look at someone who is seriously impaired and feel sorry for them, to wish they had full use of their body and mind. The truth is, every person with disability has those same feelings from time to time. This attitude is not harmful if used sparingly, like a spicy seasoning. But when pity is the predominant attitude, there is little room to see the true fullness of an individual's life. That person might have a very loving family life, or a sharp sense of humor. They may find much joy in music, or watching movies. Remember, people with disability do not experience themselves as disabled all or most of the time. They live their lives as best they can, just like everyone else. And, just like everyone else, they have days when everything looks sour, and any other life looks better than their own.

When someone is pitied, a natural reaction is to feel shame. With the abundance of pity they receive, it is understandable that those with disability would commonly feel ashamed of their bodies, both in appearance and behavior. Shame occurs when one can't help being who one is. It differs from guilt, which arises when someone has done something wrong and is aware of the mistake. There are those who cannot help stuttering, drooling, stumbling, needing to wear diapers, exhibiting uncontrollable arm movements, having unattractive features, etc. Unlike discomfort, which is a mild feeling, shame goes deep and is extremely difficult to relieve or transform. Dissolving the attitude of shame in people with disability could take several generations of people who are committed to changing these harmful perspectives in themselves and their children.

There is a fine line between pity (sympathy) and compassion (empathy), but the difference is significant. Pity feels sorry for the victim, and sees him or her as "less than." Like fear, pity identifies the person with their lacking abilities. Compassion is when a person's life is recognized not only for the struggles and afflictions, but also for its integrity, even in extreme circumstances. Feeling compassion requires honoring the life and experience of others, even while feeling their pain and loss. There's no need to fix them or make them different from what they are. Acceptance of their challenges is actually a great gift for them, a true support, because they are being seen as real people, not stereotypes. Pity is black and white: if you don't have a disability, that's good; if you do have a disability, that's bad. Compassion is all shades of gray: there are many possible roads through life, and each one has value. Pity leads to charity, while compassion leads to enablement and protection of rights. Compassion finds a way to acknowledge the seeming contradiction of strength and weakness existing simultaneously in a person.

An Exercise in Imagination

Now that you have had a chance to explore some common attitudes and what lies behind them, take a moment to imagine this scenario, in which you are the star.

> Picture yourself in a supermarket, on line at the check-out counter. Ahead of you is a young man, who is obviously mentally retarded. He is with an older woman who appears to be his mother. Your first impulse was to choose another line, but you decide to try your new attitudes, so you smile and say hello. He looks at you, but doesn't answer. He makes a guttural sound, nothing like a word. His hand jerks and waves. For all you know, he might be upset with you. He makes the sound again, and now you see he is trying to say something to you. You say, "Pardon me?" He repeats the sound, but it still makes no sense. Again you say, "What did you say?" You find yourself a bit annoyed that the mother is not paying any attention or helping her son communicate with you. You realize you are not going to understand him, so you smile and nod, telling him, "I'm sorry, I don't understand what you're saying." Remind yourself that it is okay not to understand, that all communication is not verbal. Remind yourself that you are connecting with him by a caring attitude, and that words are secondary. You congratulate yourself on overcoming the fear and discomfort; that was the primary intention. Good work!

Teachers as Role Models

Teachers must never forget or underestimate the effect of their words and behaviors on students. Attitudes and values are taken in by students even on a subliminal level. It is crucial that teachers not only examine honestly their deepest attitudes about disability, but that they consciously work towards a healthy and sensitive approach. Only in this way will they communicate the intended message. The two following stories illustrate how teachers can unknowingly affect their students' attitudes.

During a disability sensitivity presentation in a fifth grade class, a teacher raised her hand to share a story about meeting a little girl with a large growth on her face. The teacher went on and on about how sorry she felt for the child, hardly able to look at her. Standing behind the little girl on a check-out line, she forced herself to look into the little girl's eyes, in order to avoid looking at the growth on her cheek. She was surprised to see that the little girl was quite cheerful, totally unaware of the facial imperfection or the teacher's repulsion. Even though she could see that the little girl was happy and loved by the mother, the teacher communicated to her class only a sense of horror and pity for the child.

In another presentation, we were encouraging students to smile and say hello to people they meet who have a disability. The teacher spoke up to say that many people with disabilities have rude, angry attitudes, and maybe it's not such a good idea to talk to them. We were surprised to hear this, as it seems to be a rare incident. However, the class was probably more influenced by their teacher's negative words than by our suggestions to be friendly.

These stories show how a teacher's casual, even well-meaning, remarks can impress children with the wrong message. Their feelings and comments were honest and based on personal experience. However, neither of them seemed aware of their underlying feelings of fear and pity. In the first case, a teacher could speak about how she feels sorry for the little girl, and ask how she might get past that attitude in order to be more friendly and open towards her. She can still address feelings of pity, while acknowledging her need to move past those feelings into the larger context of the child as a whole person, someone who deserves friendship. In the second case, the teacher would have done better to support the presenter's suggestions of saying hello and smiling, with an added reminder that if people are not being friendly in return, do not persist.

The teacher's opinion is probably the most important one for the students to hear. For this reason, teachers need to be very careful about how they present their viewpoints. To change the way one speaks about disability takes a conscious effort. When there is discomfort, the solution is to look at it and ask how can one be more accepting, less frightened. Attitudes follow intention. Reading this book is an excellent first step in becoming worthy role models for students regarding disability. It may take some time and practice, but it's possible for everyone. The best reward is the feeling of comfort and friendliness with people who used to "turn us off."

A Few Things to Remember

In summary, here are a few points to remember in learning how to become more aware of underlying attitudes and develop more appropriate and accepting behaviors in interactions with people who have disability.

1. It's natural to feel sorry for someone who has a severe impairment. Don't beat yourself up for feelings of sadness when you see someone who has a serious impairment. If you are a caring person, you are likely to feel badly for someone who cannot do much. The problem comes when pity defines the individual as pitiful. A person's life may be very different or unusual, but it's still worth living, it's still of value. You can feel sorry for someone and at the same time appreciate the life he or she leads. Don't let feeling sorry get in the way of friendliness.

2. It's natural to be attracted to beauty and repelled by deformity. This is an unconscious human trait. Lovely images are reproduced by great artists; beauty is enjoyable and inspiring. On the other hand, it is a natural response to turn away from disfigurement. However, a real person lives inside the physical strangeness, one who often experiences fear, rejection, and loneliness. When attitudes remain unconscious, those with different bodies and behaviors are avoided. By increasing media awareness, the limitations of the "Hollywood" standards of attractiveness can be brought into focus with awareness, and not blindly accepted as the rule.

3. It's natural to want to look at someone who looks or acts different. Like everything out of the ordinary, disability both repels and fascinates. You are not a rude person if you have the desire to look at someone who is different! This is completely natural, and does not have to make you feel uncomfortable. It's more polite to look openly at someone, wearing a smile on your face and nodding or saying hello, than to purposefully look away. If done in an open, friendly way, looking at someone can be a way of communicating acceptance. If done in a guilty, secret way, it communicates pity and rejection.

4. No one chooses to have a disability. Each person living with disability is doing his or her best to live a full and meaningful life. If they could change themselves to be fully able, they very likely would make that choice. Every one faces the possibility of becoming permanently or severely disabled, and the chances increase with age. Regardless of what challenges are dealt to a life, support and acceptance of others is crucial to achieve individual potential. The more we are able to look at the content of a book, not just its cover, the more comfortable we will feel with people who are different on the outside, but not very different on the inside.

Self-Assessment Survey

The following survey is intended for both teachers and students, both with and without disability. Teachers should complete the survey before using it as a class activity or discussion starter. This survey has only one intention: to help the person completing it to become more aware of his or her personal attitudes regarding disability. While the questions are direct and revealing, they are not meant to trick you in any way. *There are no right or wrong answers!*

Take some time before the survey to stress the importance of giving thoughtful, honest answers. Do not have students put their names on the survey, because that could discourage truthful answers. If there are too many "positive" responses, your students may be trying to present themselves according to their ideas of correctness or kindness. The best answers are the most honest answers. Only by looking closely at unconscious or unnoticed attitudes, will change be possible.

Check as many answers as apply to you.

1. When I see a person in a wheelchair that appears to be mentally impaired as well, I feel
   - _____ afraid.
   - _____ embarrassed.
   - _____ like crying.
   - _____ like laughing.
   - _____ like staring at them.
   - _____ like talking to them.
   - _____ like looking away.
   - _____ sad.

2. People who have severe disability sometimes
   - _____ are not capable of communicating.
   - _____ don't notice other people.
   - _____ are more friendly than most people.
   - _____ would rather be left alone.

3. I feel uncomfortable around people with disability, if I don't know them, because
   - _____ I might say the wrong thing.
   - _____ I might hurt their feelings.
   - _____ I might injure them.
   - _____ they look strange.
   - _____ my friends will tease me.
   - _____ they can't talk to me.
   - _____ they won't understand what I say.
   - _____ I might catch a disease.
   - _____ they act strange.
   - _____ I'm embarrassed about being able-bodied.

4. What I know about disability comes from
   - _____ someone I know personally who has a disability.
   - _____ television shows.
   - _____ movies.
   - _____ reading about them in books or newspapers.
   - _____ things I've heard from other people.

5. When I think about disability
   - _____ I wonder what it would be like to be very different from everyone else.
   - _____ I think those people should be put into institutions for their own sake.
   - _____ I hope it never happens to me.
   - _____ it makes me feel scared, but I don't know why.

6. People who use wheelchairs usually
   - _____ are mentally retarded.
   - _____ can't work at jobs.
   - _____ are very nice.
   - _____ don't have many friends.
   - _____ have people at home who help them.

7. When I see someone who has a severe disability, and looks and acts very different, I think
   - _____ he might be dangerous.
   - _____ she will probably grab me if I go too close.
   - _____ I'd like to talk to him but I'd better not.
   - _____ that person is just weird, and I don't want to deal with her.

_____ maybe he needs help.
_____ I wish I knew what to say to her.

8. I feel sorry for people who have a disability because
    _____ they can't do all the things I can do.
    _____ they're probably unhappy because of the disability.
    _____ they don't get to do anything fun.
    _____ other people make fun of them.

9. When I'm around someone who has a disability, I feel embarrassed because
    _____ I can do a lot of things they can't.
    _____ they might be jealous that I don't have a disability.
    _____ it's not fair that they have a disability.
    _____ sometimes I make fun of people like that when they're not looking.
    _____ I don't know what to say to them.

10. When I hear someone making jokes about people who have disability,
    _____ if it's funny, I laugh.
    _____ I tell them to stop.
    _____ I don't say anything, but I feel bad about it.
    _____ I have some good jokes to share, too.
    _____ I think it's okay, because we're not telling it around a person who has a disability.

11. It's okay to tell jokes about people with disabilities because
    _____ they don't really understand, anyway.
    _____ I tell jokes about other kinds of people, too.
    _____ they shouldn't let it bother them.
    _____ the jokes aren't about one specific person.

12. The thing I'd like to know about disability is
    _____ how people come to have a disability.
    _____ what it's like to live like that.
    _____ how to talk to someone with a disability.
    _____ whether I should offer to help, or not.
    _____ how I might hurt people's feelings or insult them with-out knowing.
    _____ if the person with the disability is angry at other people about their condition.
    _____ why some people have disabilities and others don't.
    _____ why kids with disabilities come to school, even if they can't read or write.
    _____ how I can feel more comfortable when I meet someone who has a disability.

Myths and Misconceptions

People with disability are saints.

How often people with disability are put on an unrealistic pedestal! They are seen as exceptionally strong, courageous, outstanding or honorable. They are thought to be especially wonderful people, because they have been tried and tested by life. Yes, they do have many challenges to deal with, but all in all their lives are as special and as ordinary as anyone else's.

People with disability are sinners.

Some people think that disability comes from doing something wrong, or living an evil life, or having parents that did something wrong. As a result, that person is bearing the punishment for being bad. Disability is the result of genetic and hereditary causes, injuries and accidents. Disability is present in people of all walks of life, good people, nasty people, rich and poor, old and young, crossing all boundaries and distinctions. It is ignorant and naive to think that all these people are being punished for wrongdoing.

People with disability are pitiful.

It is commonly thought that having a disability leads one to have a lonely, unfulfilled life, because no one wants to be around those within disability, except the people who are paid to take care of them. People who have disability actually lead widely varied lives that can be surprisingly full of fun, friendship and personal achievement.

All people in wheelchairs are mentally retarded.

This is a good example of a superficial judgment, with no basis of fact. Disability has such a range of type and severity, that it is hardly ever appropriate to make assumptions of this sort. Only by meeting an individual can one know exactly the limits and expressions of their abilities.

People with disability are disgusting.

While this may sound harsh, there are indeed many people who have this type of attitude about someone who is physically deformed or incapable. The fact is, some disabilities cause bodies and facial features to be highly unattractive. The individual did not choose to have a disability, and cannot help being unattractive. They need acceptance and friendliness as much as, or more than, everyone else.

Aware of Our Words

Inappropriate: "If that happened to me, I'd kill myself!"
"He suffers from multiple sclerosis."
"He is confined to a wheelchair."
Disability-first language:
"The disabled student...."
"The handicapped woman...."
"That boy is crippled."

The term *handicapped* is considered by some to be degrading, since it probably derived from a term for beggars, "cap in hand." While still generally accepted, it has been mostly replaced by use of the term *disability*.

Appropriate: "Living with a disability must be awfully
challenging."
"His disability is multiple sclerosis."
"He uses a wheelchair to get around."
People-first language:
"This student has a disability."
"The woman has a handicap."
"The boy has a disability that affects his
walking."

Most people would not be insulted to hear the terms *disabled student* or *the student is disabled* rather than *the student has a disability*. However, learning to use people-first language helps us to think in a different framework: disability is something that someone has, not who they are.

Ideas for Discussion

1. Shame

Discuss what shame feels like, and situations where students have felt shamed by someone. Compare the difference between shame, embarrassment, and guilt. When someone has made you feel ashamed, what are your feelings toward that person? Ask the same question about embarrassment and guilt. Do any of these feelings create anger or fear? Ask the students to examine their own attitudes toward friends and siblings. Can they see ways that they shame others?

2. Body Image

Ours is a "beautiful body" society. Have your students discuss how they become aware of standards for physical attractiveness. What are those standards? Have them give examples of media attitudes, marketing strategies, and peer pressure. What feelings underlie having a "less than perfect" body? What is it about themselves that they don't like, or would wish to change? Discuss the fact that they cannot change certain things about themselves, and how that compares with someone who must live with a disability.

3. Disability in the Media

Have your students think of any famous people with disability that they are aware of. How have they learned about these people? In what ways does the media promote or degrade images of certain groups of people? Have them discuss various ways they have seen people with disability portrayed in movies, novels, or television shows. Have students share stories about people in their families who have experienced short- or long-term disability, and how that experience impacted their own lives.

4. Self-assessment survey

Have each student each fill out the survey. Assess the completed surveys by compiling the answers on a master survey (see Lesson Plans below). Especially note questions where a majority of students gave the same response, which will indicate a generalized attitude. This is a good place to begin a discussion of students' fears and discomforts around disability. What situations have they witnessed, in school or otherwise, where someone with a disability was teased or mocked? Help them to examine their own reactions when they have felt left out or rejected by peers. What feelings did they experience? What actions did they take? Also discuss ideas for getting more exposure to people with disability. Have them talk about students with disability in your school. What do they know about them? Do they know their names or their disabilities? Discuss ways they might find out about a peer student who has a disability.

Lesson Plans

Photo Pages (Grades 4 - 12)

Objective: To introduce students to an actual person with a severe disability, and to inform them about his or her life.
Timeframe: Two class periods or interspersed with other lessons.
Steps:
1. Have the students divide into small groups. Each group is given a photo card of Menard. One student is chosen to read aloud the information on the back of the card to the other group members. Allow approximately 10 minutes per card per group. (For younger elementary students, the teacher may present each card to the entire class, holding it up for display while reading the information on the back, then passing it around the class.)
2. Have each group write out several questions they have about the picture on the card before passing it on. They may ask about any aspect of Menard's life. Some of their questions may be answered when they look at the other cards, but this exercise will help stimulate their ways of looking at disability. Another suggestion is to have them jot down words that come to mind, without thinking first. Instruct them to "turn off the internal censor" and be spontaneous in their responses. Reassure them there is no right or wrong; the goal is to be honest about attitudes.
3. After 10 minutes, each group passes their card to another group and the exercise continues. Teacher: take notes on any comments you

might overhear that indicate student's feelings about seeing the reality of Menard's life. Without identifying who made the comment, it can be used for future discussion time, to begin eliciting attitudes and emotions that surround severe disability.

4. During class two, bring out the cards again for a whole class discussion. Go through the questions on the back of each card. Have the students present any unanswered questions they had from Step #2. If their questions cannot be answered by information in this chapter or on the cards, consider inviting a professional speaker to the class (see following lesson plan).

5. Word lists. Review the word lists from Step #2. Are there any words that the students no longer feel comfortable using? Discuss why.

Guest Speaker: Person with a Disability (Grades 4 - 12)

Objective: To develop empathy and awareness in students through a personal encounter with an individual with disability.

Timeframe: One to two class periods.

Steps:

1. Locate a person in your community who has a disability and would be willing to speak to your class. Possible ways to find such a person include: ask students if they know someone who would be appropriate; inquire with other teachers or your special education staff; contact a local association or agency such as the Association for Retarded Citizens (ARC) or an independent living center. You will want to find someone who is able to speak well, and is receptive to the idea of educating young people about disability. It is recommended to find someone through a reference who knows the individual personally, rather than just ask someone you don't know.

2. Spend some time prior to the presentation to inform the students about the speaker, and what he or she will speak about. Encourage the students to think about any questions they might have beforehand.

3. Allow the speaker a full class period, even if he or she is finished earlier. Have the students write the guest a thank-you letter.

Art project: Magazine Collage (Grades 4 - 12)

Objective: To increase students' awareness of media literacy issues regarding the use of bodies in advertising. To promote students' awareness of the lack of representation of disability in advertising.

Timeframe: Two to three class periods.

Steps:

1. Have the students gather old magazines and newspapers that can be cut apart.

2. The students' task is to find magazine ads and photographs depicting society's standards for physical appearance. Point out how women and men are shown in seductive poses to sell items that have nothing to do with romance or sex (e.g. cars, cigarettes). Also have them look for the common standards for physical attractiveness in models, and how body parts associated with sexuality are often the focal point of the photograph (buttocks, breasts, legs, etc.).

3. Using the photos and captions collected, the students will make a large collage which exposes the marketing strategies of advertising. The collage can be posted in a school hall.

4. Spend some class time discussing what the students found. Did any of the ads particularly surprise them? How do they feel personally when they compare themselves to the standards? Did they find any ads that showed someone with a disability? If so, what was the context of the ad? What was the type of disability?

Media Literacy for Older Students (Grades 10-12)

Objective: To increase students' media literacy with films, in regard to portrayal of disability.

Timeframe: This project can range from an individual class period to a semester-based unit.

Steps:

1. Have your class view one or more of the following movies, with the intention of observing how the person with a disability is portrayed, and what issues are presented. The movies are grouped below according to type of disability. You might also use the help of a local video salesperson if you have questions.

2. Students may write a report on the film(s). Some thought-provoking questions to address include: How was the person with the disability treated? What were his/her feelings about the disability? What type of message does the film give to viewers about someone in this situation? Did you get a sense of this person as a real person? Do you think the story was realistic?

3. Use the "Ideas for Discussion" section in this chapter for class discussion after movies.

Some contemporary movies you might use include:

Movies about paralysis (spinal cord injury)

Discussion ideas: What are the challenges of adjusting to disability in later life? How would your values change? your needs? your fears? your dreams? How does disability affect issues of sex, intimacy and friendship? Where and how are these issues dealt with in the films? What are the overall themes of the movies, positive or depressing?

• *Coming Home* (rated R) A Vietnam vet paralyzed during the war is trying to adjust to his life and values back in the United States.

• *Born on the Fourth of July* (rated R) A young man goes to Vietnam and gets paralyzed. Similar theme to *Coming Home.*

• *Passion Fish* (rated R) After becoming paralyzed, a young woman struggles to learn how to use her body. Very realistic story about physical rehabilitation and friendship.

• *Waterdance* (rated R) Slow-moving, realistic story of a young man who is paralyzed and in a rehabilitation center.

Movies about other physical disabilities

• *Nightmare Before Christmas* (rated PG) A cartoon movie that depicts the evil scientist in a wheelchair. Discussion: How will a movie like this form a young child's view of wheelchair users and people in similar circumstances?

• *Forest Gump* (rated PG-13) Forest Gump has an intellectual disability. He is teased and taunted by childhood friends. Supporting character Sergeant Dan loses both legs in Vietnam, and goes through a period of extreme bitterness, anger and self-destructiveness. Discussion: What are the realities of adjustment to life with a disability? What are the reactions of others to Forest? to Sgt. Dan?

• *Children of a Lesser God* (rated R) A teacher at a school for young people with hearing impairments falls in love with a student with complete hearing loss. The story includes the current emphasis on (and resistance to) teaching lip reading and speech to hearing impaired students. Discussion: what would life without hearing be like? Would students want to learn lip reading and speech? Why did the starring actress resist? How does disability impact intimate relationships?

• *My Left Foot* (rated PG) Life story of Christy Brown, an Irish author and painter with cerebral palsy, based on his autobiography. Beautifully acted film illustrating the importance of family and community support in reaching personal potential. Discussion: How was Christy accepted and involved in his family and neighborhood in ways we rarely see today? How did his family's support help him to move beyond his limitations? How would his life have been different if he lived in an institution? What was Christy's experience of having a severely limited body and a fully functioning and creative mind?

Movies about mental illness and retardation

Discussion ideas: Family issues of caring for someone with a mental impairment. What feelings do the characters have about the person with the disability: frustration? anger? resentment? love? protectiveness? Identify scenes for different reactions. Consider how the different aspects of a person may or may not be affected by mental impairment: intelligence, friendship, ability to earn a living, ability to care for someone, artistic talents, sense of humor, communication, technical skills, etc. What kinds of rights are individuals with mental disability entitled to have?

• *What's Eating Gilbert Grape* (rated PG-13) Gilbert Grape's younger brother is mentally retarded, and his mother's obesity makes mobility a serious difficulty for her.

• *Bennie and Joon* (rated PG) Two mentally ill young people meet and fall in love.

• *Slingblade* (rated R) A man with mental retardation is released from long-term hospitalization into a small community.

Media Literacy for Younger Students (Grades 4-9)

Objective: To increase students' media literacy with films, in regard to portrayal of disability.

Timeframe: Two to three class periods.

Steps:

1. View the movie *Nightmare Before Christmas* with your class. A good preparation for this activity is to have a brief discussion about what it's

like to meet someone in a wheelchair. Ask your students what sort of people use wheelchairs. You could also administer the Self-Assessment Survey as a preliminary activity.

2. Discuss the doctor character. What were their reactions to him? Did they like him? Did they find him frightening? Was he a "good guy" or a "bad guy"? Ask your students what the movie teaches little children about people in wheelchairs.

3. Have your students prepare a small blurb about the disability attitude demonstrated by the film. A short paragraph is sufficient, one that notifies future viewers of a negative role model. It should be worded in an inoffensive, informative manner.

4. Contact your local video rental store and ask if the blurb can be attached to the video, so that when customers rent the movie they will have a few sentences to make them aware of the negative attitude being communicated in the film.

5. Discuss with your students how this small effort will inform many people of an attitude that would normally go unnoticed by most viewers. Their project could change people's ways of thinking! (Note: even if the video stores are unwilling to attach the blurb, the exercise will educate students in communicating this type of information to others.)

Graphing the Self-Assessment Survey (Grades 7 - 12)

> **Objective:** To teach students how to compile data into visual graphs and tables, to increase awareness of overall class attitudes about disability.

Timeframe: Two to three class periods

Steps:

1. Collect all the completed surveys from class members. Have a blank survey form to use for compiling the answers. For each question, count the number of responses for each line. Fill in that number on a blank survey form. (Note: Students were instructed to mark as many responses as applied for them, or they might have left some questions blank. If students checked more than one response, the number of responses for the question will add up to be higher than the number of students completing the survey. If some students did not answer some questions, the number of answers will be less than the number of students.)

2. For each question, count the number of responses on the collected surveys. Fill that number in on the blank form.

3. Divide each response total by the total of answers given, to get percentages.

4. Example for Question #1:

When I see a person in a wheelchair that appears to be mentally impaired as well, I feel

__5__	afraid (10%)	__9__	like staring at them
__7__	embarrassed (14%)	__6__	like talking to them
__2__	like crying	__10__	like looking away
__0__	like laughing	__9__	sad

Total answers given: 48   Total students in survey: 36

First response: afraid: 5 (students marking that response) divided by 48 (total answers given for the question)= .10 or 10%

Second response: embarrassed: 7 divided by 48 = .14 or 14%, etc.

The total percentages should add up to 100 percent. (If there is a half percentage, such as 14.5%, round it up or down as necessary to make the total equal 100%.) It won't matter if some questions have 48 responses and some have 36 and others have 29. The total of percentages should always equal 100 percent.

5. Now you have percentages for the class answers. For example, 14 percent of the class feels embarrassed.

6. There are different ways the information can be charted. It can be written out by question, with percentages filled into the blank spaces. It can be turned into pie charts, with the question written below each pie. It can be made into bar graphs with the questions written at the bottom of the graph, and the bars rising to the appropriate percentages listed vertically.

7. These results can be made into large poster displays for other classes to see. Or the class may want to administer the survey to several classes and compare results. Perhaps the results from a class that includes a student with disability will be different than from a class that has not been exposed to special education students.

8. The students may want to create their own survey with different questions, and compile those results.

Student Biography: Menard

2.1: Menard

Sixteen-year-old Menard has a disability that was caused by serious heart problems. He was born with several holes in his heart, which made it difficult for the heart to pump blood. This situation was life-threatening, and needed to be repaired with open heart surgery. But during the surgery something went wrong, and Menard's heart stopped pumping for a few minutes. Since blood carries oxygen to all parts of the body, this meant that the brain did not get oxygen, and as a result Menard's left side was partially paralyzed and lost feeling. Lack of oxygen to the brain is called a stroke, and often results in this type of nerve damage on one side of the body.

Figure 2.1 Menard (photo by Bob Blair).

Although Menard did not walk until he was four, in many ways he grew and developed normally. His right arm and leg are strong; his left arm and leg are thin and weaker, and his left wrist wants to curl up because he doesn't use that hand very much. When Menard walks he appears to be off-balance. He lifts up high on the right leg then lowers down on his left leg. He can run, but it looks crooked. Menard's speech is slurred when he speaks too fast, and sometimes people have to ask him to slow down or repeat what he said. When speaking slowly, he is very easy to understand.

The disability doesn't limit Menard very much. He looks and walks a little different, but in general is very much like any other teenager. But the disability has given Menard courage. He's been through many challenges, such as serious surgeries. He faces his life with a brave spirit, does not lie to others or himself, and is very slow to anger or get upset. His weakened heart carries a risk of death; Menard knows this but continues to have one of the most joyful smiles you'll ever see.

Questions:

1. Have you ever tried getting dressed or doing a job with just one hand? Do you think it would be frustrating?

2. Since Menard lost feeling in his left side, what are some dangers he has to be aware of?

3. Why do you think challenges in life make some people brave and others timid? How do you respond to challenges?

2.2: Shooting Hoop

Menard's favorite sport is basketball. For some strange reason, his disability made him grow very tall, so this is the perfect sport for him. He wanted to play on the school team, but his disability prevents him. For one thing, it would be hard for him to compete against boys who have full use of their arms and legs. Another problem is that too much running is hard on his heart. Even though his heart was repaired, it is not quite as strong as a healthy heart. He spends a lot of his free time practicing shooting.

The basketball coach came up with a solution for Menard: this year he will be the manager of the high school team. He will help take care of the equipment, run errands, and attend practice. He will be required to go to all the games with the team, a job he is very excited to have.

Figure 2.2 Shooting Hoop (photo by Bob Blair)

Menard stays very active and is always looking for something to do. At home he reads, rides his bike, listens to music, and talks on the phone. He can fix his own meals. He will be able to work and support himself once he graduates from high school. He'll be able to have his own home, walk to work or ride a bus or bicycle, cook for himself and pay the bills. His adult life will be very much like everyone else's.

Questions:

1. Do you think being team manager will help Menard feel included in the team, or will it make him feel more left out because he can't play?

2. What kinds of adult jobs might Menard do when he graduates, using one hand?

3. Menard has to take care of his body in special ways that most young people don't even have to think about. What are some of these ways?

2.3: In the School Store

Menard takes care of himself fully when he's at school. He doesn't need help to get around or eat. He can carry his own lunch tray in the cafeteria using his one good hand, and visits with friends who do not have disabilities. Because he is mentally able to do school work, Menard spends a lot of time with general classes, not just in special education. He is very friendly and happy, smiling a lot, joking, and wanting to meet people.

Every day, he works in the school store, selling things, making change, and stocking the shelves. The money part helps him with his math skills. Because of his friendliness, Menard would make an excellent store clerk when he graduates. He also likes the idea of getting vocational training to operate or repair computers.

Menard says, "Sometimes I forget I have a disability. I never think about it unless people tease me. Then I feel like there's something wrong with me. But there isn't really anything wrong—I'm just different." It's hard for him, to be laughed at or teased. He can't help having the body he has, and it hurts his feelings when other kids make fun of it. Thanks to his good nature, Menard doesn't get angry or say nasty things back to them. He doesn't get depressed about his condition. He just lives his life and enjoys what he can do. It would be nice if he could go about his business and not hear insulting comments.

Figure 2.3 In the School Store (photo by Bob Blair)

Questions:

1. Do students in your school make fun of kids with disability? How does that make them feel? How does it make you feel when you see it happen?

2. How can Menard be such a happy person if he has a disability?

3. Besides being laughed at, what other things might remind Menard of his disability?

2.4: Physical Therapy

Menard spends much of his school time in the Resource Room, where students get special teaching help. Teachers work with Menard individually on math and reading. His disability is fairly mild, so he has no problem communicating with others. However, his brain was affected by the stroke he had as a baby, and so he hasn't been able to learn quite as well as other students his age. He takes regular classes in Business Math, International Cuisine (cooking) and Shop. He reads at a junior high level, which means he can read and understand books, magazines, and newspapers. He enjoys reading in school and at home. His favorite book is *Chicken Soup for the Soul.*

Figure 2.4 Physical Therapy (photo by Bob Blair)

Menard also receives physical therapy during school. The therapist works to strengthen his left arm and leg. In the photo, she is helping Menard work with his arm and hand. He is lying on a support called a "wedge," which holds up his body so he's not lying flat on his face. While leaning on his elbow, the therapist helps Menard open his wrist, since it tends to curl. She has to work slowly and gently, a little each day, to keep the muscles from getting tighter. If someone were to pull back hard on his wrist, it would hurt. The therapist also helps Menard strengthen his left leg and develop his balance for walking and running. Without this type of exercise, Menard's body would weaken and become stiff.

Questions:

1. Why doesn't everyone need physical therapy? How do most young people stay healthy?

2. Do you think it's harder to have a disability when you have the mental awareness to know people are teasing or rejecting you? Is it easier or harder to be mentally unaware of your differences?

2.5: Woodworking

Over the years, Menard has learned to do many things using just one hand. For example, he works in the wood shop at school, using hand tools and palm sanders. He doesn't use the electric machinery, like table saws, because he has to be very careful not to injure his hands. Using a power saw with one hand could be very dangerous. Instead, he works on projects with classmates who help him with the parts he can't do. He's not ashamed to ask for help when he needs it and he doesn't get angry if people offer to help.

Menard can also ride a bike with one hand, and swim. He dresses himself, feeds himself, and in general takes care of himself completely. He lives with his father and two brothers. He likes going to the movies with friends, most of whom do not have a disability. He's a "cool" kid, wearing fashionable clothes and listening to popular music. He baby-sits for younger children to earn some spending money.

Menard is especially friendly and kind, and often helps other students in the special ed classroom where he spends part of his day. Some of his classmates cannot walk well, or they use wheelchairs. Menard is strong enough and healthy enough to help other students go up stairs, or push their wheelchairs. He often does errands for the teacher as well. He also takes the time and makes the effort to communicate with students who have more severe disabilities.

Figure 2.5 Woodworking (photo by Bob Blair).

Questions:

1. When you think of people with disability, do you think of them as getting help from others or giving help to others?

2. When you see someone walking very lopsided, what's your first thought about them?

3. Knowing that Menard is happy, and knowing that Menard has a disability that makes his life more limited than yours, do you feel sorry for him? Explain your answer.

Chapter 3

CAUSES OF DISABILITY

W e live in a cause-and-effect world. We want answers. We are taught to believe that for every phenomenon there is an explanatory cause. Years, decades, and millions of research dollars are spent researching the *"why"* of every conceivable detail of our physical environment.

When it comes to disability, cause and effect are not simple. Many disabilities have multiple causes; many have unknown causes; still others have secondary conditions, that is, one disability causes another. However, when someone is obviously so different, the thought occurs, "What happened? Why is he like that? Could it happen to me or my children?"

Looking at causes is a way to begin understanding the nature of disability. The topic is addressed in two sections. The first part attempts to put cause in its proper perspective, by examining how (a) causes range from simple and classifiable, to complex and unknown, and (b) knowledge of causes is less important than knowledge of the disability itself. The second part of the chapter outlines several categories that explain the more common ways disability happens to people. These are very general groupings that are described in lay terms, intended to give the reader a realistic framework for thinking about the origination of disability.

Some Things Cannot Be Known

An essential component of the medical profession concerns diagnosis, which is accurate much of the time. Proper diagnosis contributes to correct treatment. Sometimes diagnosis is clear-cut: colds and flu are caused by bacteria or viruses; headaches or back pain can be caused by stress; a severe fall could result in broken bones. Medical science has even determined that certain foods and substances can cause cancer and heart disease. Cause and effect: do *this* and *that* happens. But some areas of medicine are not so obvious. Disability is infinitely varied in how it is caused and how it will manifest in an individual.

Imagine a child with cerebral palsy. Perhaps it was a difficult birth; the labor was traumatic, and during the procedures there was a shortage of oxygen to the baby. Soon after birth, it is determined that the child sustained brain damage, and now has cerebral palsy. What would the cause be? If the cause was the difficult delivery, why was it difficult in the first place? Or if the cause was oxygen deficiency, there is still the question of why there was a shortage of oxygen. There is also no way of knowing if the child would have been born with cerebral palsy even in an easy delivery, resulting from some other cause during pregnancy.

Several teenagers are out on the town. They drink some beers while driving around listening to the radio. On the way home, they pick up speed, the driver loses control, and the car crashes into a telephone pole. One of the young men has a broken back, which injures his spinal cord; he is paralyzed. The simple answer is that the paralysis resulted from the spinal injury. Some people would consider alcohol part of the cause, at least a contributing factor. One could also say the driver's lack of control led to the injury.

A one-year-old child is diagnosed as developmentally delayed. The 27-year-old mother was healthy throughout her pregnancy and delivery. The child has received regular medical care and excellent nutrition. There is no history of this type of problem in either parent's family. All areas that would usually be checked for cause appear to be normal. What is the cause? It is clinically listed as "unknown."

These questions apply to almost every incidence of disability. Even when a cause seems apparent, there are additional, underlying factors that are integrally related to the occurrence of the disability. There are no simple answers for why people are born outside the "normal" range of development, or develop disability after birth or later in life. Nonetheless, even knowing this does not keep us from *wanting* a simple answer, and perhaps making assumptions that are very likely incorrect.

What Needs to Be Known

A good perspective to develop when examining disability is that *cause* is secondary in importance to *effect*. The *effect* is the fact of the disability: what are the person's capabilities, limitations, special needs, future prognosis? How can he or she function today, at home, in the classroom, or in society? What kind of communication is possible? What level of learning and development is possible? What quality of life is possible? The *cause* does not change the nature of how the situation will be handled. It is purely past information; it may or may not be of use or interest in the present, which is where the actual individual exists. The *effect* determines everything about our relationship with a person with disability.

While a correct diagnosis is crucial, it does not always contribute to the treatment of the disability. Diagnoses indicate how the condition will present itself, including the limitations and potentials for the individual. Some disabilities are progressive, meaning that the individual will continue to lose mental or physical abilities over time. Other conditions may improve noticeably with therapy or other treatment. All of these factors affect how an included student will participate in a general classroom, and how interactions with other students will evolve and grow.

It is also important to know that many disabilities can be prevented with proper education. Students can benefit throughout their lives by learning about the actual dangers of drinking and driving, inadequate prenatal care, and child abuse. By receiving information now, they can come to understand that certain conditions are passed along genetically, and that they may have a choice to make or a chance to take within their own families. The section below addresses different areas of prevention that can be applied to several disabilities.

Perhaps the one allowable assumption in any case would be: *the individual did not choose to have the disability.* This general rule of thumb focuses us on the fact of the disability, rather than the cause. Recognizing that an individual must live a difficult and challenging existence encourages compassion and eliminates blame. By reflecting on how easily it might have happened to ourselves, or a loved one, chances are good that there will be less desire to avoid the one to whom it *did* happen.

Healthy Curiosity

Despite these precautions against giving too much weight to the cause of disability, there may still be a need to know about cause. This chapter is meant to dispel confusion and misconceptions. Knowledge, even if it means knowing there is *no* answer, is better than ignorance, basing an incorrect answer on a personal assumption.

It is certainly possible to find out the true cause of a students' disability. Ask questions, and take the time to identify and clarify clinical names. A student's special education teacher or classroom therapist (speech, physical or occupational) will probably know how the disability originated. Once you look at several complete stories, you will begin to see that each case is remarkably unique. The biographies throughout this book also provide a wide range of samples. Taking a proper approach to cause eliminates the need to lump together any and all disability into a misconceived explanation.

Following are several categories of causes. They are not necessarily technical or clinical descriptions. The intention is to provide a basic foundation in understanding some of the more frequent ways that physical, sensory, emotional and cognitive functioning become impaired.

Disability Present from Birth

When disability is present from birth, many people will label it as birth trauma (something damaged the developing fetus) or birth defect (how that particular fetus developed). These terms refer to the fact that the disability originated prior to or during the time of birth, or very early in life, during the developmental stages of the brain.

There are numerous reasons why a disability might be present from birth. The most common explanations include: injury or disease during pregnancy, drug use during pregnancy, hereditary factors, environmental factors, complications during delivery, and unknown causes. These causes can have similar results in terms of outcome, or can vary. For example, use of certain drugs by the pregnant mother can produce skeletal deformities or mental impairment in the baby, or both, or neither. Each of these categories is described more fully below, along with types of disabilities likely to result.

1. Congenital Birth Defects

The term congenital means that the child was born with the condition. Causes can stem from factors in the fetal environment (the mother's womb) or they can actually be unexplainable. Cleft palate and clubfoot are two manifestations of congenital birth problems.

• *Unknown reasons.* Sometimes a fetus develops a deformity, not necessarily because of a hereditary factor or anything that occurred during pregnancy. This type of disability is usually referred to as a birth defect. Birth defect is an overly generalized term that some professionals consider outdated. The term is best known in conjunction with fund raising telethons and appeals, where every conceivable disability is grouped under that one label. If those organizations had to be more specific, the list of their children's disabilities would fill textbooks! If there is no medical diagnosis for a disability, it is more correct to say "unknown" than to identify "birth defect" as a cause. Sometimes a pregnant mother lacks proper vitamins or other nutrients, which can contribute indirectly to an inexplicable condition in the baby. Prenatal care is one of the most crucial areas for prevention of disability present from birth with no explanation of cause.

• *Drug use by mother.* Drug use by a pregnant woman can cause serious damage to her baby. Many prescription and over-the-counter drugs, as well as illegal substances, are known to affect the proper development of the nervous system and the physical structure of the fetus. Perhaps the most famous case of this type of environmentally-induced damage was thalidomide, a drug given to pregnant women for nausea. Babies were born with severe skeletal abnormalities and missing limbs. Accutane, a prescription drug for acne, is also known to cause birth defects if taken during pregnancy. Use of alcohol can lead to fetal alcohol syndrome, which impairs cognitive functioning. Many of these products carry warning labels, which are of extreme value in preventing unnecessary and undesirable effects on a fetus. Use of so-called recreational drugs such as LSD, cocaine, or marijuana also carry strong elements of risk for pregnant women. Besides avoiding toxic substances, choosing a healthy diet is crucial in preventing a baby's disability during pregnancy. Lack of proper nutrition in the mother deprives the growing fetus of nutrients essential to full development.

• *Exposure for mother.* When a pregnant woman is exposed to certain environmental toxins, the effects can reach her baby, resulting in skeletal alterations or brain damage and mental retardation. Radiation in the form of x-rays is one way that a developing fetus can be damaged through the mother's exposure. Technicians regularly ask female patients if they are or might be pregnant, in order to protect their abdominal region from harmful rays. Insecticides have also been determined to be dangerous. The linkage of insecticide exposure with certain birth defects has led to boycotting movements among farm workers.

• *Disease in mother.* Certain viruses, when contracted by a pregnant woman, can have damaging effects on the baby. These viruses include Rubella (German measles), herpes, HIV or AIDS, or other unknown strains that may cause a high fever during pregnancy. High fever in the mother can result in brain damage to the child. German measles used to be a common cause of mental retardation, before a vaccine was discovered that could eliminate that danger.

2. Genetic/Hereditary Causes

The term genetic means having to do with genes, which are the biological elements that determine every aspect of an individual, from hair color to height and weight, from intelligence to athletic ability and artistic talent. This genetic code is carried by the DNA, which is present within the developing fetus. Genes provide the blueprint for the growing organism, and account for the differences and resemblances among generations of family members or anyone related by descent. There is a very precise way that genes are structured, and if this arrangement is altered, the result is an abnormality in the baby's development.

Two types of genetic mutations can occur. The first is called hereditary, when the parent is known to carry the gene that causes a certain condition to run in that family. However, the occurrence of the condition even within that family can be unpredictable. There is a chance a child in that family will be born with the condition, but no guarantee. Some conditions have a higher percentage of occurrence than others, and many can be tested in the parents to discover if they will pass it on to their children. Medical science has made enormous advances in this field, thereby preventing conception of children who will have severely disabling conditions. Genetic counseling can save families from a lifetime of emotional and financial strain that goes along with caring for a completely dependent child.

The second type of genetic disability occurs randomly, with no evidence in prior generations of the defective gene. Once manifested, this type of genetic occurrence may or may not be passed on to future generations, depending on the particular situation. In general, genetic disabilities are not always predictable.

Probably the most familiar disability stemming from genetic causes is Down's Syndrome. The genetic mutation occurs in the mother. Occurrence of Down's Syndrome is often, but not always, influenced by age; an older mother will be more likely to produce the abnormal gene structure. At age 25, a woman has a one out of 2,500 chance of having a baby with Down's Syndrome. By age 45, her risk has increased to a one out of 30 chance. Another genetic disability is muscular dystrophy. This condition is a gender-linked disability, as the condition is carried in a woman's gene and passed on to male children.

3. Oxygen Deprivation

Oxygen deprivation is a main contributing factor to many congenital disabilities. The term *hypoxia* refers to decreased oxygen supply, while *anoxia* means no oxygen. A wide variety of mishaps can accompany a baby's delivery, causing the baby to end up without sufficient oxygen. The result will be some degree of brain damage.

The brain requires an enormous amount of oxygen to function properly. Oxygen is delivered to the brain by the blood vessels. If the supply of oxygen is interrupted even briefly, either because the patient stops breathing or the heart stops pumping, brain cells begin to die. Five to six minutes without oxygen can have irreversible effects on the brain, and ten to twelve minutes is almost always fatal. Depending on the section of the brain affected, disability in one or more areas will result.

Oxygen deprivation is one piece of the cause rather than a cause in itself, since there is usually, although not always, an underlying reason for the deficiency. Effects of oxygen deprivation can include: mental retardation, brain damage, seizures, paralysis (stroke), speech and language dysfunction, and visual impairment. The most common disability associated with brain damage (not necessarily resulting from oxygen deprivation) is cerebral palsy.

Cerebral palsy is a catch-all term applied to a broad spectrum of conditions that exhibit an abnormality in the central nervous system. A significant number of children in special education programs are identified as having cerebral palsy. Pediatric neurologists disagree on the use of the term, because of its vagueness. However, most professionals will still use the term cerebral palsy to classify any brain damage that occurs during the prenatal stage, during delivery, or immediately after, and doesn't continue to get worse. Clinical manifestations vary from a mild limp with normal intelligence, to severe dysfunction of all limbs, speech, swallowing, and mental impairment. It's interesting to note that some individuals with extremely impaired motor functioning may have above average intelligence: active and able minds trapped in bodies that cannot speak or hold a pen.

4. Birth Trauma

Birth trauma refers to stressful situations that can arise during or prior to delivery. This is another tricky area, since it can never be known for certain if a difficult delivery caused damage to the baby, or if the baby was already carrying a weakness that created a stressful delivery. Birth trauma encompasses such situations as distress of mother or baby during labor and delivery, injury to the mother during pregnancy, oxygen deprivation, and surgical mishaps.

5. Unknown Causes

Regardless of how a disability appears, whether it is mild or severe, there is no guarantee that the cause is known. Many severe and profoundly limiting conditions are actually comprised of multiple disabilities. Some of them may have an explanation, others may not. It is surprisingly common to have "unknown" as the clinically documented source of a disability. These conditions arise for no apparent reason.

Disability Occurring Later in Life

A great number of permanent and severe disabilities occur well after the infancy and developmental stages. Many of them result from causes similar to those originating at birth: environmental toxins, lack of oxygen, or trauma. Some common disabilities become apparent in adult years, such as multiple sclerosis. Other examples of debilitating conditions include Parkinson's and Lou Gehrig's diseases, which affect the nervous system, and degenerating conditions that affect eyesight and hearing.

1. Trauma/Injury (Postnatal)

Injury is an extremely common cause of disability in our society, for children and adults alike. Injuries leading to permanent or severe disability are usually to the brain, spinal cord, or skeletal structure. Serious trauma or damage to the brain or spinal cord is often irreversible. Depending on the location of the injury, the condition will involve paralysis and/or brain damage, which may manifest in a variety of ways. Injury to the skeletal structure may result in amputation or chronically impaired use of limbs. Injuries are commonly referred to as accidents.

• *Spinal cord injury* affects all or part of the body, according to the level of the injury. *Paraplegia* refers to paralysis of the lower limbs (anywhere below the chest level); *quadriplegia* refers to paralysis of all four limbs. Sometimes a person with quadriplegia will have partial use of hands, arms and shoulders. If the injury is in the upper neck region, respiration can be affected as well, requiring assistive devices for breathing and neck support. Paralysis is most commonly caused by automobile collisions, sports injuries, and gunshot wounds.

• *Head injury (traumatic brain injury)* can damage the brain while leaving the physical functioning unharmed, or it can impact the nervous system throughout the body in a variety of ways. This type of injury can be as mild in its effect as slight memory loss, or as severe as complete loss of cognitive awareness and physical control. Statistics indicate that 99,000 people a year sustain moderate to severe brain damage, 50 percent as a result of automobile collisions.

Information and awareness can help reduce the numbers of people left permanently disabled by injuries. This category is very applicable to students, who are typically active and generally see themselves as invincible. The high incidence of car accidents is directly related to drug and alcohol use, and a disproportionate number of young people sustain spinal cord and head injuries as a result.

2. Environmental

Environmental causes cover several areas of concern in the field of disability. As explained above, the developing fetus is directly affected by anything ingested by the mother in the form of foods, drugs (both prescription and illegal), and other substances. Once born, the child is subject to other dangers in its external environment, which exist in toxic and harmless objects alike, and also within the psychosocial environment of the family.

• *Child abuse and neglect.* Emotional and/or psychological deprivation or abuse can result in mentally retarded or emotionally disturbed children. Children who are diagnosed as "failure to thrive" can sustain lifelong damage due to the lack of proper mental and/or physical stimulation and nurturing during critical developmental periods. Shaken Baby Syndrome, a form of physical abuse, can be so severe as to cause brain injury or death. While technically injuries, these situations fall outside the conventional definition that would ascribe injuries to accidental causes.

Child abuse and neglect is a growing area of awareness and concern. Clinical studies have reported on the long-term damage sustained by children who are victims of this type of environment. Special education departments across the country are being swelled by numbers of children diagnosed with emotional/psychological disturbances and impaired mental functioning, originating in abusive home environments.

• *Oxygen deprivation resulting from accidents or injuries.* The effects of lack of oxygen to the brain (see above) are as serious to children and adults as they are to infants. Since hypoxia is usually related to an accident or injury, it can be considered environmental in nature. In later life, brain damage can be caused by aspiration (breathing in a foreign object which obstructs the lung passage), electrocution, surgical mishaps, carbon monoxide poisoning, near-drowning, or any situation that involves interruption of the heart's beating.

• *Poisoning.* Environmentally, people are exposed daily to a variety of dangers, from simple household cleaning substances to food poisoning to radiation fallout. The results of poisoning can be devastating and lifelong. Many toxic substances have been removed from the market in the United States, but not in less advanced countries. Lead-based paints and insecticides are two examples of poisons that caused numerous disabilities before being outlawed or controlled. Mining exposure and air pollution continue to affect numbers of people with respiratory conditions and birth defects.

Environmental disability has the greatest potential for prevention. Proper prenatal care for pregnant mothers can identify and prevent many potentially problematic areas in the developing fetus and during birth. Education about the effects of toxic substances, especially the use of drugs and alcohol, is another effective area of prevention.

3. Disease

Disease is another way that people can become disabled in later life. This used to be a more common cause, as many disabilities originating from disease have been eradicated due to vaccinations. Polio, a virus that causes paralysis, was once of epidemic proportions in our country, and today is an extremely rare occurrence; measles was another virus common to children that had the potential of causing brain damage and blindness. Diabetes and heart disease remain two of the most disabling diseases in our country. In general, owing to the advances of medical science, permanent disabilities resulting from disease have been significantly reduced.

Summary

Still, we wonder why. These differences in people illustrate the infinitely varied ways that human beings are packaged. Abilities manifest in a bell curve: some have more, others have less; the variations are endless. Each individual expression exists within the whole and serves a purpose, however obscure. Nonetheless, cultivation of an attitude of acceptance, with or without an explanation, will help each of us learn a greater appreciation for the rich texture of life created by differences among people.

Myths and Misconceptions

His mother must have taken drugs.

It's surprising how many people think mothers are the sole cause of a child's disability. As the chapter explained, this is only sometimes the case. Even if the disability is congenital, there are often other causes than mother taking drugs or being irresponsible.

She was born with it.

This might be a correct answer, but once again, if it's an assumption, there is no way of knowing. Some very severe disabilities develop later in life, and progress to very serious stages of limitation.

It's contagious.

A contagious disability is a rare thing. If a person has a disease that is contagious, which causes impairment of physical or mental functioning, it would probably be labeled as a disease rather than a disability.

People with disability are especially fragile.

This may or may not be true. You probably can't hurt someone by pushing their wheelchair or offering an arm if they are unsteady on their feet. If they are very fragile, chances are good that they are protected from harm, e.g. wearing a helmet or leg braces. It's appropriate to ask if you are unsure, "Will I hurt you if I help you in this way?"

If someone can't speak, they can't think, feel or understand.

Some people with profound disability of muscle control and speech have full use of their mental abilities. It's not unusual for individuals that look very different to actually be extremely aware and intelligent. Even if they can't respond, they are listening and understanding.

Aware of Our Words and Actions

Inappropriate:	"What happened to you?"
	"What's wrong with your child?"
	"It's so tragic, he might as well be dead."
Appropriate:	"May I ask what your disability is?"
	"I've never understood why some people end up with disability and others don't."

Just a simple hello, with eye contact, directed to the person with the disability and their companions/caregivers.

Ideas for Discussion

1. Safe childcare

(a). Students caring for students. Discuss baby-sitting practices and care of younger siblings with your students. What do they need to be aware of in a young child's environment? In a child's behavior? How serious can the results be of an injury, or a child breathing a piece of food into his or her lungs? Discuss levels of responsibility in caring for a child. Let the students share stories of their own experiences guarding children from dangerous situations.

(b). Abuse and neglect. This topic is a frequent news story. Even though these issues are common knowledge, we may never realize the long-term effects of severe abuse and neglect. Discuss the following dangers to young children:

• Shaking a baby. A baby's brain is not fully developed at birth, leaving a space between the brain and the skull. When a baby is shaken violently, the brain gets smashed against the skull bone, and damaged. The brain damage can show up immediately, or years later. Swinging a child by the wrists can cause shoulder dislocation. Young bones are still forming, and the entire structure is more fragile than that of a grown body.

• Inadequate nutrition. A baby's rate of growth is accelerated, and the body needs many vitamins and other nutrients to ensure proper development both physically and mentally.

• Lack of attention. Without the stimulation of language, eye contact, emotional and physical nurturing, the human organism fails to grow in normal patterns of development. Studies are relating psychosocial behaviors and emotional disturbances with conditions of neglect or abuse in early childhood.

Explore the differences between accidents that happen to young children, and abuse inflicted by an adult. Discuss the implications of parental responsibility in protecting and caring for children.

2. Prevention

As the chapter explained, many serious and permanent disabilities can be prevented. Discussion of this issue can focus on drugs and alcohol, a familiar topic among students. These issues face them in the media, in their families, and in school. Have they ever realized why they are told *"Just Say No?"* What are some of the possible effects of drug use before pregnancy? during pregnancy? after pregnancy? Are there damaging effects from tobacco use during pregnancy? What is the responsibility of the child's father during the mother's pregnancy? Discuss common causes and elements of prevention for injuries, birth defects, genetic disability. What steps can young people take to protect themselves and others from possibly disabling sports and car accidents? How does a young woman find out more about proper care during pregnancy, before she is pregnant? Suggest that your students share this information with their parents and siblings.

3. Sharing

One of the best ways to open up discussion of disability is to have students share who they know that has disability, and to tell about their experience with that person. How is that person different? How is that person similar? Guide the discussion towards feelings and relationships. Create a list of feelings that arise when students see a person with a severe handicap. Throughout the discussion, pay attention to students' use of words describing or identifying someone with a disability. Point out any biased remarks as they arise, thereby helping students become more sensitive with their words. Create a list of derogatory names that students have heard or used about people with disabilities.

4. What if?

Ask "what if?" questions to get a discussion generated. For example, what if your brother or sister became disabled? A parent? A friend? What would the adjustments be for you and your family? How would you feel? Who would you go to for support? How do you think different people would react? What if you yourself became disabled?

Who would you talk to about it? How would your life change? What would you miss most? Feelings can go in many different ways around this issue. Take the time to fully explore students' emotions such as fear, guilt, anger, blame, in an imaginary or real situation.

Lesson Plans

Photo pages (Grades 4 - 12)

See Lesson Plans in Chapter 2 for guidelines to using the photo pages for this chapter.

Guest Speaker: Professional (Grades 4 - 12)

Objective: To obtain factual knowledge about disability from a professional in the field.
Timeframe: Three class periods.
Steps:
1. During one class, talk about causes of disability as presented in this chapter. Follow with discussion based on one of the ideas above. Have the students develop a list of questions regarding causes of disability.
2. Invite a professional speaker, such as a doctor, special education staff member, or physical therapist, to visit your classroom and talk about causes of disability.
3. Have the students write an imaginary scenario of a person becoming disabled. Remind them to give details based on facts they have learned about a disability and its causes.

Warning label survey (Grades 4 - 12)

Objective: To familiarize students with the use and value of warning labels.
Timeframe: Two to four class periods.
Steps:
1. Spend one class period discussing prevention of disability, as in Ideas for Discussion.

2. Assign the students to take an inventory of various products that carry warning labels. Include: medicines, cleaning substances, ointments, alcoholic beverages, cigarettes or tobacco, etc. Their lists should name the product and describe the effects warned against. For example, beer bottles carry labels warning against use by pregnant women, because of the possible danger of birth defects.

3. Allow a few days or a week for the students to prepare their lists, since it will involve going to a store. If possible, take a field trip to a large supermarket that includes a pharmacy and liquor section, and gather the information at one time. Class can break into small groups and each take a certain section of the store.

4. Have the students prepare a master list on a large poster that can be displayed in the classroom or school hallway to inform other students. They can draw or cut out magazine pictures of dangerous products to decorate the poster.

Creative Writing (grades 4 - 12)

Objective: To develop sensitivity awareness; to enhance understanding of an individual's challenging situation; to practice creative writing skills.

Timeframe: One to two class periods.

Steps:

1. After viewing the photo cards of Maurice, have each student write a short story titled "A Day in the Life of Maurice." The story can be from the perspective of Maurice, or one of his parents or brothers. It should include one or more of the following elements:

• Description of some aspect of taking care of Maurice
• Feelings about living with Maurice
• Description of a communication with Maurice
• Something that happened in the family or in school. It can be funny, scary, sad, etc.
• Traveling somewhere with Maurice

2. Have the students read aloud their stories. Each story will reveal different angles of Maurice's life, and students can learn a lot from each other's perspectives.

3. Note: Younger students may prefer to draw pictures of Maurice in his wheelchair or on his bed, Maurice's house or bedroom.

Parking Lot Guardians (grades 4 - 8)

Objective: To increase students' awareness of disability parking space violations, to increase community awareness of disability parking space laws.

(This is a good assignment to follow a guest speaker presentation.)

Timeframe: One class period.

Steps:

1. Have the students come up with one or more designs for a "ticket" that can be used for cars parked illegally in a space designated for drivers with disability. The ticket should be several inches square, with printing or type on one side only. It should be simply and politely worded, for example: "Did you notice you are parked illegally in a space reserved for drivers with disability?" or, "Parking in this space requires identification on your car—do you have a disability?"

3. Print the tickets on colored paper, 4 to 6 tickets on an 8 1/2" x 11" sheet of paper. Cut the sheets of tickets.

4. Each student gets a number of tickets to take with them. The students need to first check and make sure a car does not have proper identification for disability status before giving out a ticket. Disability status is shown by a placard hanging on the rear-view mirror, or sometimes laid on the dashboard, or else with a license plate with a disability symbol on it. Certain military veteran license plates have disability privileges also. Tickets should be placed under the windshield wiper of cars parked illegally, with the printed side facing in to the driver's seat.

5. This could be a field trip project if your school is nearby a large parking lot. Or students can use their tickets on weekends and report back if they found any violators.

6. Students can also research how many disability parking spaces are required by law within a parking lot.

Student Biography: Maurice

3.1: Maurice

Maurice is 20 years old, and lives in Taos Pueblo, a Native American village in New Mexico. He lives with his parents and two brothers, and attends public school daily. At school, Maurice lies on a high bed, which is more like a padded table. Teachers and students talk to him and take care of him.

Maurice was born a healthy baby. When he was almost two, he was playing with his cousins, running around the house. He put a peanut into his mouth, laughing and running, and suddenly the peanut went down his throat and caught. He choked, but instead of coming up, the peanut went into the lung. After a few weeks, he got very sick. He was taken to the hospital for an operation. The doctors used a long, thin instrument to reach into his lung and pull the peanut out. But during this procedure, something went wrong and Maurice stopped breathing several times.

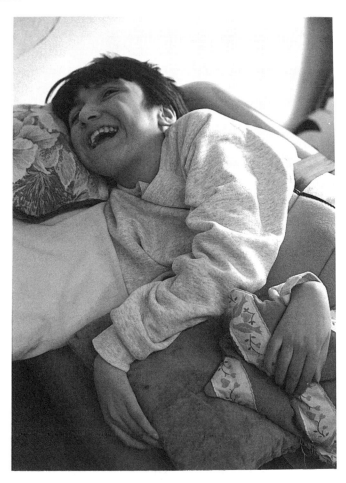

Figure 3.1 Maurice (photo by Bill Davis).

When someone stops breathing, there is no fresh oxygen coming into the body. The brain needs enormous amounts of oxygen, which is carried by the blood. When the brain doesn't get the oxygen it needs, brain cells begin to die. Depending on where the cells die, an area of the body will not be able to work properly. Almost all areas of Maurice's brain were damaged. Because Maurice stopped breathing for a long time (a total of 7 minutes), his brain was severely damaged. He became completely disabled, so that he cannot move any part of his body except his eyes, and cannot speak. We have no way of knowing how much Maurice is aware of in his surroundings.

Questions:

1. Think about what it would be like to take care of Maurice every day. What kind of feelings would you have? Would your feelings change sometimes?

2. How are some buses equipped especially for wheelchairs or people who can't climb the stairs to get on?

3.2: The Grasshopper

Maurice's body is very stiff. He cannot move any part of himself voluntarily. Because he is not moving around, keeping all his muscles loose and stretched out, they have become tight. You can see that his hand is very bent at the wrist, and his feet point upwards by themselves. This picture shows how he lies in a frame called a "grasshopper" that holds his legs in different positions during the day. Since he cannot move his muscles, they have atrophied (become shrunken), so his entire body is very thin. Maurice's mouth stays open because he doesn't have control over opening and closing it.

Maurice communicates discomfort by moaning. One day Maurice moaned for several hours before a teacher happened to take off his shoe and found a marble! It had probably fallen into his shoe at home before it was put on his foot. No one knew why he was moaning until the marble was found and removed–then he stopped. We know Maurice can hear because when someone comes up to him and says hello and claps their hands above his face, he smiles. When Maurice smiles, it is like a gift to us, because it is his only way of communicating his pleasure. This is how he shows that he hears us, and that he knows someone is with him.

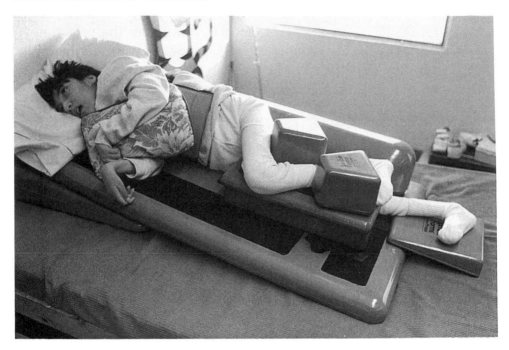

Figure 3.2 The Grasshopper (photo by Bill Davis).

Questions:

1. How would you communicate with Maurice if he were your classmate?

2. Doctors, teachers, and family make sure Maurice does not gain much weight. How would being thin be helpful to Maurice and the people that take care of him?

3. When Maurice is moaning, what might be going on in his mind? How does your body let you know when you are in pain—by thinking or feeling or both?

3.3: Family Time

Maurice goes everywhere with his family, including the pow-wows that are held at the Pueblo. Many other Native Americans come from other locations to have a great celebration with drums, dancing, ceremonies, and lots of food. Maurice and his family also go out to restaurants, but they must always find one that is accessible for Maurice's wheelchair. Although it is a very difficult challenge for Maurice's family, they have kept him at home rather than putting him in an institution for people with disability. They have given him a wonderful quality of life through their willingness to take care of him.

Maurice has two brothers. Tristan says that when he is frightened, he lies down next to Maurice. He believes that Maurice protects him from bad things. Tristan and Michael talk to Maurice, even though he doesn't answer. He is very much a part of their lives. Maurice's brothers like to take their toys and play on his bed, even putting the toys on his body.

Figure 3.3 Family Time (photo by Bob Blair).

Michael reports that sometimes other boys will try to hurt him by saying, "At least I don't have a retarded brother!" This does hurt Michael, because he loves Maurice, and knows that Maurice can't help being the way he is. Michael doesn't think it's a bad thing to have a brother like Maurice.

Questions:

1. Why is it a difficult challenge for Maurice's family to keep him at home?

2. What are some of the things they have to think about or plan for with Maurice?

3. How would Maurice's life be different if he were in an institution? Do you think he would notice the difference in his environment?

3.4: Lunch Time

Everywhere Maurice goes, he must be carried or pushed in a wheelchair. His family gets him dressed in the morning, and ready for bed at night. He cannot help at all, by lifting a leg or pushing his arm through. It's almost like dressing a doll. They bathe him, comb his hair, and brush his teeth. He is fed through a tube that goes directly into his stomach through a small incision. It doesn't hurt him at all. The food is in a liquid form that has all the nutrients he needs. In this picture, the woman is holding the feeding tube. He used to be able to eat through his mouth, but now he never tastes his food. It goes into his stomach and keeps him alive, but he doesn't ever take it orally. He is not able to swallow properly, so if he had food in his mouth he could breathe it into his lungs and choke. Maurice cannot control his bladder or bowels, and so he wears a diaper.

Questions:

1. Have your parents ever told you not to run with food or objects in your mouth? Why?

2. What were some of the feelings Maurice's parents might have felt when they found out that he would have a severe disability for the rest of his life?

3. Do you think Maurice's family ever wishes he might have died peacefully during the operation? Would you?

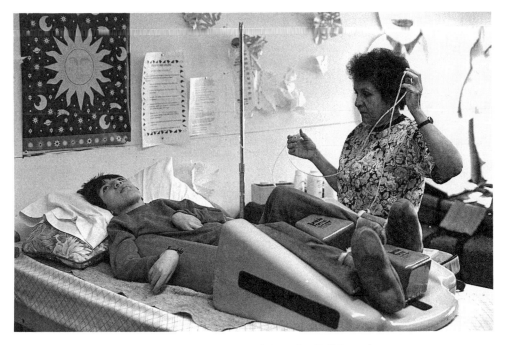

Figure 3.4 Lunch Time (photo by Bill Davis).

3.5: Getting Leg Braces

Every day, therapists at school move Maurice's legs and arms to keep them from getting stiffer. This photo shows two people fitting Maurice for his leg braces, which help his legs stay straight. These professional workers are very gentle with Maurice and are not hurting him, even though his face looks unhappy. He might be uncomfortable, but we can't be sure. People that work with Maurice always tell him ahead of time what they will be doing. They never treat him like an object.

Some people think that since Maurice cannot respond, they don't need to bother with him. But even though he's not able to do anything for himself, he's still aware on some level. He lets us know by smiling or groaning that he has feelings. When visitors come into his classroom, they are encouraged to say hello to Maurice, instead of ignoring him because he can't say hi or talk to them.

By thinking about Maurice's life, it helps us feel grateful to have the abilities we do. We can feel appreciation for the health of our brothers, sisters, parents, relatives, and friends. It's up to us to treat people like

Maurice the same as we would treat someone who has full use of their body. It's okay if he doesn't say hello. He hears it being said to him, and so he is included.

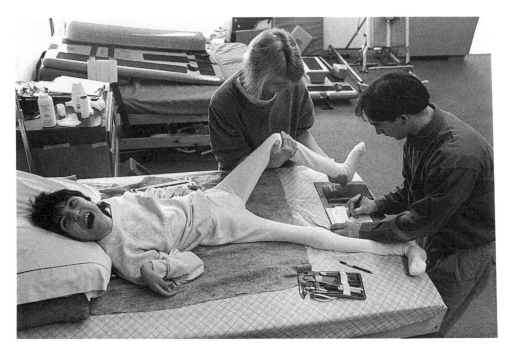

Figure 3.5 Getting Leg Braces (photo by Bill Davis).

Questions:

1. What is it like for you when you say hello to someone and they can't respond?

2. Why do most people feel uncomfortable around someone like Maurice? Do you?

Chapter 4

FAMILY ISSUES

When a student with disability enters a classroom, he or she brings along more than the ordinary student in terms of family involvement. Often the teacher will need to be informed on a host of issues stemming from the student's home life and family situation. A teacher's understanding, insight, and sensitivity to the student's out of school circumstances will greatly aid successful integration of the student within the class. At times, the family may be looking to the teacher for support and advocacy for their child's education.

In order to function effectively as a team, teachers and parents need to develop a working relationship built on open attitudes and conscientious listening skills. The teacher's responsibility includes learning how the family feels about their child's disability and education. Do they support inclusion in the classroom? How do they handle medical and social questions? Are there siblings at home? Who provides primary care for the child? These are some of the many details concerning the family's way of life with a child with disability. A teacher who knows the student's family will be able to assist them in making decisions and providing the best quality education possible for their particular child.

Raising and caring for a child with disability demands a level of dedication and acceptance beyond the normal parenting role. Even a child with minor special needs requires additional effort by the family to obtain proper care, education, and support. Those with more severe disability often need a range of services and therapies, much of which is supplied by family members. This type of involvement in a child's growth and development often places extreme demands on both parents and siblings, on a daily, ongoing basis.

As you read this chapter, we urge you to imagine yourself in the shoes of the parents who are raising a child with disability. Try to empathize with the situations faced by a mother or father in these very difficult and challenging circumstances. To develop an understanding for the families you will be working with in school, it is important to go beyond the surface of information, whether in these pages or in what is presented by a parent, and seek a heartfelt insight from which to offer support and possible solutions.

A Kaleidoscope of Issues

Families caring for a child with a moderate to severe disability commonly have an increased stress load physically, emotionally, socially and financially. Of course, each family is unique in handling their situation, and also in the kind of support they might need. Some families have virtually no discipline problems with their child, but may have greatly increased levels of care giving. Other families may be dealing with difficult behaviors from a child who is completely physically capable.

The following issues outline general areas of focus for a family living with a child with disability. Each family's needs are unique, and must be considered on an individual basis. However, looking into the kaleidoscope of issues that come along with disability helps us to form realistic attitudes and responses about that particular type of life.

Economic Issues

Most people have experienced the anxiety caused by financial insecurities in this day and age. From time to time, everything seems to fall on us at once, enough to tip the balance towards a deficit and keep us awake at night scheming how to make ends meet. For the family of a child with disability, many aspects of life are magnified. Financial responsibility is one of these aspects. Increased cost of living is often a permanent pressure, stemming from various specialized needs, such as:

• increased medical involvement, illness, periodic hospitalization, therapies

• adaptive/assistive equipment

• adapted family vehicle or special van for transport of manual or electric wheelchair

• accessible or adapted housing: ramps, thresholds, room space
• paid respite care providers

Children who are clinically diagnosed with a disability, mental (cognitive) or physical, are often eligible for government subsidized programs for medical support, treatment, and equipment. Supplemental Security Income (SSI), a branch of the Social Security Administration, provides monthly cash benefits and medical coverage for people with disability. Under SSI, a child receives a Medicaid card which covers all, or a substantial portion of, basic medical costs from doctor visits to prescription drugs to surgery to adaptive equipment. Some states sponsor programs that provide support in specific areas for children under the age of 18. SSI and many other available benefits are "means tested;" in other words, eligibility is based on the family's income until the child is 18, at which point eligibility is based on the grown child's income. It is worth noting that the cut-off line is usually quite low, making these benefits applicable mostly to lower income families while the child is a minor. However, many middle income families qualify because the exorbitant costs of medical services for a child with disability, which are tax deductible, reduce a family's income to within the range of eligibility for state and federal benefits.

This can be a frustrating situation for families who can afford general living costs, but not the high costs of medical care for the child. Medical coverage may be all they really need, but even a comfortable middle range income can exclude them from such help. Many adults who live with disability cannot afford to be employed because of costly medications or treatments. They could not hope to find a job that pays enough to cover these costs, and so choose to remain unemployed in order to keep receiving the medical aid.

When a family does not qualify for aid, they have very few alternatives for meeting the potentially excessive costs of their child's care. Some financial assistance programs exist which offer one-time aid for specific equipment or treatment. Families may need to meet stringent requirements, and there is no guarantee that their request will be approved. Even after a time-consuming process of obtaining a doctor's order and having the child measured or evaluated by a physical therapist (which may involve travel as well), the request can be denied. In many cases, the child must do without a piece of equipment that could be extremely valuable in terms of quality of life, but is not critical to the child's health or safety. One family single-handedly raised over

$20,000 in their community to purchase a specially adapted van for their teenage son, who uses a wheelchair. They wrote letters, held bake sales and other fund raising events, and approached every community group and club available. They were successful, but it was an enormous effort for all involved.

Another additional expense for families is that of paid respite care for their child. Since many of these children require specialized care, families cannot hire a teenage baby-sitter, as they might for a child who does not have a disability. Parents may have to pay higher fees to have someone stay with their child if they want to take a trip or even go out for an evening alone. The prohibitive cost of skilled care impacts the parents' social life as well, as even a night out for dinner and a movie can be expensive as well as difficult to arrange.

Social Issues

Social life for a family is almost always limited, to a greater or lesser degree, by the presence of disability. Every aspect of life outside the home, that is, life within a society or community of people, is magnified by disability. While it is not necessarily impossible, a satisfying social life requires extra effort for these families and/or individuals. Social issues include:

- family outings
- vacation travel
- educational and social activities for the child with disability or for other siblings
- parents' time together
- parents' time separately for individual interests and personal friends

Family outings, even as simple as eating out, must often be planned in advance to account for accessibility in restaurants, motels, theaters, zoos, etc. Entrance accessibility, bathroom dimensions, and rest areas are some of the details to be determined. Some families must consider how far they will be from medical assistance, or carry along necessary supplies for a possible emergency. A child who tires easily will affect the limits of the entire family. Many families choose their activities based on how much effort will be involved; the child's needs are the determining factor for the type of activity, entertainment or vacation. Parents who make the dedicated choice of including the child end up relinquishing much of their personal freedom in order to give their child the highest possible quality of life. This can be a permanent way of life, as many parents of children with severe disability care for their children for twenty, thirty years or more. The complexities of life required to live with and care for a child with disability reflect the commitment and sacrifice that these parents offer their children on a daily basis.

Families also face the public attitudes described in Chapter 2: Prevailing Attitudes, when they take a child with disability on outings. These attitudes can create a sense of isolation for parents who feel that no one else really understands their situation. Criticism can come from both directions: for being too protective on one hand, and for exposing their child publicly on the other hand. Parents report being met with comments such as, "You should just keep your child at home." The individual with the disability is not the only one affected by such attitudes; parents also are vulnerable to other people's opinions about how they should handle this challenging situation.

It is not hard to imagine a family's heartbreak and anger at witnessing their child being teased or rejected. Some parents choose not to face that cruelty, and tend instead toward over-protection of their child, shying away from social activities that would only cause them more pain. These family attitudes can then hold back the child from access to healthy developmental opportunities, due to fear of public reactions and concern for the child's safety. Some of these concerns are valid and necessary, while others are a defensive reaction to hurtful past experiences.

Parents who are raising a child with disability have to make twice the effort of other parents to get their own personal "time off" from the daily demands of parenting. If the disability is severe, only specially trained respite providers will be suitable to care for the child. Even then, it often seems safer and easier to stay at home, thereby avoiding the anxiety of leaving the child, if only for short periods. If the disability is not as severe, the child is still often excluded from the usual overnight visits, parties and trips to which many able-bodied children are invited. Parents of able-bodied children usually enjoy the occasional breaks when their children are at a friend's house. That type of social interaction is rare for the child with a severe disability. It is not unusual for teenage children with disability to never have spent a night away from home without parents. The opportunities do not arise, since friendships are limited by peer attitudes and care requirements. In some cases, parents of children without disability are uncomfortable having a child with disability as a guest.

Another social issue is the question of independence for the child. Parents raising children without disability expect and welcome the normal stages of independence as the child grows, for example, when the child is first able to play independently, or go visit a relative alone. Independence continues to unfold with after-school activities, dating, and eventually moving out of the home. For the parents of a child with disability, independence is an unknown. How much will the child ever be able to do on his or her own? Prognoses are not always accurate, leaving ample room for hope as well as fear. Severe disability requires continuing care, and a lifetime of dependence can feel like an insurmountable mountain to parents of a young child looking ahead at the future.

Teachers may initially think a family is being overly concerned or involved with their child due to the disability. To understand their position, it helps to imagine the circumstances they have lived with over the years, including their efforts to function as a social entity and also as sole care givers for an especially dependent child.

Cycle of Adjustment

For every family and every individual living with a disability, there is a cycle of adjustment during which one gradually accepts the routine reality of the situation. This cycle is very similar to the cycle one goes through in grieving, because disability involves loss: for an individual it is loss of the ability to function as a peer, to join in certain activities and to be accepted by the common standard; for a family, disability can be the loss of a dream for their child, and a harsh reality at first, of what their lives will be like caring for a child with exceptional needs.

The grief cycle usually begins with anger and resistance. "Why me?" is a frequently asked question during this time. Parents who give birth to a child with a disability are often unaware during pregnancy that there is any problem with the developing fetus. Like other parents, they are planning their lives with a new baby, envisioning all the wonderful times together as a family. Pregnant mothers commonly wonder if their child will be healthy and whole, reassuring themselves that most children are indeed born healthy and whole. So if they find out after delivery that there has been brain damage or that a genetic condition is apparent, they have had virtually no preparation for such an altered picture of family life. It comes as a shock, and nothing but time and support from others can help them move on.

The stages that follow the initial "No!" fluctuate between anger, denial, bargaining (in which one tries to mentally change the situation, for example, "If this baby gets well I'll work at the state orphanage every week for the rest of my life!") and depression. How difficult it is to truly accept that the child will never be able to join friends in normal, growing up activities. "If only....If only...." keeps parents imagining their children in scenes that will probably never come true. This is an enormous loss of a dream, and parents cannot be expected to move through these stages quickly. Living with disability is a lifelong adjustment. The disability keeps one different and separate, continuing to expose the individual and the family to public attitudes, physical illness and limitation, the need for special services, and the ever-present concern for ongoing care if the parents should become incapacitated or die. Even though the daily care and relationships become routine, the disability presents enough unexpected challenges that it cannot be forgotten.

Parents of a child with disability must learn, like all of us, how to move past their own fear and discomfort regarding disability. Love is a powerful motivation, and the fact that the person with the disability is their own child makes the learning that much quicker and easier. Love allows parents to see beyond their child's limitations, to his or her abilities, however minimal. They learn to recognize how their child communicates, enjoys, and participates in life. They also learn to see other people who have disability with new eyes. They look for other parents who share their circumstances, often joining parent organizations that are active in advocacy rights.

The adjustment takes time in every case, and what parents need most is understanding and support. They do not need to be rushed into acceptance. They need to have their feelings of anger and discouragement validated and affirmed. They may even be shocked and horrified at their own feelings of wishing the child had died or that they had never gotten pregnant. These are natural emotions that are common to the stages of grief. It does not indicate that the parents are incapable of caring for the child. They are being honest about their pain and loss. Occasionally, people get frozen in a stage of grief, most commonly in the denial phase. It becomes difficult for that family to allow their child to fully explore his or her potential; in their refusal to accept the disability, they ultimately hinder the child's development and exposure to new things.

Over time, these feelings will usually change and lessen. The day-to-day requirements continue: getting the child dressed, fed, bathed, year after year. Of course, at a certain point it becomes routine, not something that is a daily focus for disappointment. They begin to grow more comfortable in the care procedures. In the case of a birth disability, they begin to see that there are ways to communicate with the child, even if those ways are very different from the norm. With an injury, the family gradually relaxes around the new condition, whether it is a wheelchair or a brain injury requiring adaptive communication. It becomes "family life" in its own unique expression.

Emotional Issues

Over the years, the cycle of adjustment slows down, moving through wider and wider processes of grief and loss. However, the heartbreak never completely ends, and neither does the hope for a miracle. Even when a family has reached a stable level of acceptance, there will be periods of grief arising from the disability of their child. These periods often occur when the child would have been passing a milestone in life, were he or she not limited by the disability. Examples of growing up milestones include first words, first steps, joining Little League or Girl Scouts, school graduations, and religious ceremonies. Parents are often keenly aware of their child's age and where he or she would be developmentally, were it not for the disability. *He would be learning to drive; she would be swimming and bike riding with her mother; he would have been helping his father in the workshop by now; she would have been baby-sitting for the neighbors.* These types of thoughts are inevitable, and they bring with them recurring emotions of sadness and loss in a family's ongoing cycle of adjustment. For those involved with the family, understanding these cycles and learning to be compassionate and supportive will help the family move through each stage as they continue to love and appreciate their child.

It is also natural for parents to have emotions of resentment and frustration from time to time. Everyone gets just plain "fed up" with life, at times when everything seems to be going wrong. Parents who are dealing with an increased stress load as a result of caring for a child with physical, psychological, or cognitive limitations, will naturally reach a limit of giving. Their limit may be far beyond most parents', but it does exist. It's important to remember that when a parent brings a child into the classroom one morning, with the comment, "He's all yours!" it probably means, "I'm really tired today." A teacher's answer might be, "I can hardly imagine what it's like to parent a child like William. You do such an excellent job, it's not surprising that you get tired sometimes. He's a very lucky child to have you."

A parent of a child with disability might seem to worry more than other parents. This could stem from the fact that the child has required an extra degree of care than other children. Illnesses and injuries hold increased risk for a child who has a disability. Parents might also worry that their child will be exposed to hurtful teasing or mocking. It is not unusual to see an elevated level of anxiety and concern among parents of this population. On the other hand, many parents of children with disability are quite advanced in lessons of letting go and acceptance. They have had to accept so much, for so many years, in so many different ways, that they have learned to relax with the whims of life's changes, and focus on enjoying what they have today.

Sibling Issues

Many students with disability have one or more siblings at home. More often than not, the siblings do not have disability. Having children with such widely varying needs presents an additional challenge for parents. While one child needs extensive home care, another might be exceptionally active, involved in sports, school, church, or other social activities. Parents must strive to satisfy the needs of all their children, and can be overloaded with driving one to sports practice or play rehearsals, and another to doctor visits and physical therapy.

Siblings of a child with disability have a unique life experience, growing up with a brother or sister whom they love and accept as a family member, but whose needs can often interrupt their own lives.

Sometimes the siblings will not get as full access to parental support as they might want, because the parents must allocate their time and energy among all the children, including the one with extraordinary needs. The choice of family outings may be limited as to where they go and how long they stay. Since siblings know the daily routines of care, they may shoulder the responsibility for baby-sitting when the parents need to go out. Siblings can be victims of vicious teasing and hurtful remarks directed at their brother or sister because of the disability. Naturally, there are times when the siblings will feel resentment towards the child who has extreme needs, for taking too much attention from parents, embarrassment over uncomfortable public reactions, and sadness at the loss of a playmate or peer. But children who are raised with disability in the family usually get the best education in disability awareness and sensitivity. They see firsthand the complete picture of their brother or sister: the limitations, the abilities, the love and the natural sibling frustrations that transcend any differences of body or mind.

During disability awareness presentations in elementary and secondary classrooms, we have found that many students have brothers, sisters, cousins, friends and relatives with disability of one sort or another. These students often respond openly and eagerly to the opportunity to talk about their experiences and knowledge regarding disability. Teachers can provide times for discussion of disability, in order to acknowledge their students' understanding and insight, and to validate family members that might be hidden or unacknowledged.

Health Issues and Physical Care

Physical health is another major area of concern for parents caring for a child with disability. Children with impaired functioning can have generally weakened physical systems, making them more susceptible to infection and contagious diseases, and less able to recover quickly. When mobility is impaired, a child lacks the stimulation of walking, running, or exercise. The lungs have reduced capacity, with breathing shallower than normal; circulation is slower, causing skin quality to be lessened. When a disease is contracted, the child may have a harder time fighting it, having a weaker immune response. Where an able-bodied child has a cold, a child with severe impairment may easily get pneumonia and end up hospitalized. Hospitalization can be a rather routine event in the lives of many families caring for a child with disability. Being routine does not make it any easier to bear. Each occurrence brings with it anxiety and the ever-present question of the child's physical ability to overcome the illness or injury.

When a child with severe disability becomes critically ill, treatment options center around the main issue of keeping the child alive. Even with the use of sophisticated life support systems, there is no guarantee that a health-impaired child will survive. Many of these children have significantly compromised respiratory systems, cardiovascular systems, and reduced immune systems, which puts them in a higher risk category. At times of illness, parents are overwhelmed by their own emotional issues regarding the child's quality of life. They are faced with decisions such as whether to actively resuscitate a child in cardiac arrest, or to provide aggressive life support measures. What about the child who is entirely dependent, with minimal communication? Because of their love for the child, a love often deepened by the profound level of giving involved, they must weigh the child's ability to enjoy life against the child's suffering. With the mosaic of issues to be considered, the answer cannot be made or even guessed at by others who are not immediately involved. These parents need understanding, supportive, and nonjudgmental responses to whatever decision is made between the family and health care professionals.

In this regard, parents must often be especially vigilant and educated about protecting their child from disease wherever possible. They must watch for the earliest signs of respiratory congestion or skin breakdowns, both of which can lead to life threatening conditions. Injuries are also more dangerous than with strong, healthy children for similar reasons. Bones can be brittle, and healing can be prolonged. Children who are unsteady on their feet may need to wear a protective helmet while growing up; those using wheelchairs often wear a seatbelt. Spasms and seizures can sometimes be violent enough to cause physical injury, and care givers, including teachers, must be prepared and informed about preventive measures. Many, but never all, of these hazards are avoided by proper education and awareness.

Most children with severe disability require an extreme level of physical care, which includes a daily effort from parents and family members. Some children must be clothed, fed, washed, and carried. They may need help using the bathroom, or they might use diapers or catheters. It can be both incongruous and frustrating, when one's child has a fully adult body with an immature mind incapable of taking care of his or her own basic physical needs. Parents must also address the child's needs for entertainment and stimulation on a regular basis: playing simple games, taking walks, conversations (even if the child cannot speak), or going to the store. Each of these efforts can be double that of the same activity with an able-bodied child. In most families, physical dependency is a developmental stage that passes with infancy and early childhood. In the case of a child with disability, this type of care is not outgrown, and can be very tiring at times, significantly contributing to the level of family stress.

For these reasons, do not be surprised if school vacations are not welcomed by the parents of a child with disability. Time off from school can mean "double time" for parents. Finding care givers for the physically dependent child, in order for parents to continue working, can be challenging if not impossible. School hours provide a professional level of respite for parents of the child with severe disability.

Sexual Issues

Many children with disability are in a high-risk bracket for sexual abuse or misconduct, a factor that is rarely discussed openly but remains a safety priority for parents. The child with severe cognitive or speech impairment is often unable to report abuse, or even comprehend the nature of the offense. Sexual molestation can be misinterpreted by the child as affection or play, rather than something wrong or dangerous. These characteristics make an attractive victim, one that can be molested with little risk of revealing the offender. A lack of understanding appropriate boundaries also puts the child in danger of becoming a perpetrator, one who molests other children or touches adults inappropriately. This is not a result of perversion or low moral standards in the child; rather, the child is unable to comprehend why certain ways of touching are not acceptable. In some cases, sexual perpetration can indicate a history of abuse for that particular child, which is then acted out upon others. Special education classes attempt to educate students with disability about appropriate sexual behavior, even if only in basic concepts. Sexual issues are a critical concern for a child who lacks cognitive awareness, and many parents feel the need to be extremely vigilant. Teachers also need to be informed of this type of potential danger within the classroom.

Long-term Care

There are some circumstances where the family is not able to care for the child with severe disability, in which case the child becomes a resident of a nursing home facility. Often these children are wards of the state, with costs being covered through state funded subsidies. The child remains the legal child of the parents, with physical custody awarded to the state. On the whole, institutionalization for children with disability has been almost eradicated through laws that make public schooling a viable option for most. Parents who can work or rest during school hours are often able to care for the child in the evening and on weekends.

One of the deepest underlying anxieties carried by families with children who have severe disability is the question of who will care for the child if anything happens to the parents. The child's parents are usually the sole source of care, which is a tremendous responsibility. Even if there is a family member who plans on taking over after the parents are gone, parents worry about the level of care their child will receive, and whether it will be equal to the love and attention they provided. Siblings may or may not be able to take over the parents' job of caring for their brother or sister; it's an enormous job that impacts any family's lifestyle. The thought of the child becoming a ward of the state, or placed in an institution or nursing home, can be deeply disturbing and frightening. On the other hand, few parents have the financial resources to guarantee personal care for their child when they are no longer available.

This concern is often unspoken, but can create a constant, if subtle, sense of fear for their child's well-being. Parents of children with disability are challenged more than most with the lesson of learning to live for today, to appreciate their child in the moment, relinquishing the expectations as well as the overwhelming fears, in order to be thankful for their child's life and what they can share.

Disability Services

Where and how does a family begin to find services for the specialized needs of their child with a disability? The answer to this question depends on several factors, some having to do with their personal situation, and some that are applicable to all families. For example, where does the family live? Are they skilled at finding their way through the bureaucratic maze? What is their income level? What are their attitudes about their child's disability, and their rights? All of these issues will affect the type and quality of services a family will obtain.

Location

Metropolitan areas consistently have a greater variety and availability of services for children and adults with disability. While there are easily as many children living in rural outlying areas, who have moderate to severe levels of impairment, living in a city has the obvious advantage of having services within reach. Proportionately there may be similar numbers of residents with and without disability in a small town or in a city. But when the numbers are added up, there will be more people with disability in a city, therefore more services to help them. The comparative ease of getting out and around makes this population more visible as well. Some of the many services found in most cities include the following:

• *Medical clinics* provide diagnosis and treatment for children, and counseling for the family on the specific disability and the most recent findings. Specialized medical services also prescribe and provide adaptive equipment: braces, wheelchairs, speech and hearing devices, physical therapy, etc. Medical supply companies are necessary for ordering and fitting this type of equipment.

• *General support services* address everything from housing to employment to educational advocacy. Many cities currently have independent living centers, agencies that focus on the needs of individuals who want to live as independently as possible, but require some assistance to do so. These centers are often clearinghouses for all kinds of information and referral, and can be extremely helpful to families who are unfamiliar with what services are available.

• *Public transportation* has become increasingly accessible since the late 1980s. The Americans with Disabilities Act (ADA, 1990) outlined a mandate for public transportation vehicles to be fitted with wheel-chair lifts over a period of several years. The law allowed older vehicles to remain in use, with lifts being included in any new vehicles purchased. Many smaller towns with public busing have not had to comply with this law because they have not added new buses to their system. In general, accessible public transportation is only available in the larger cities of the country at this time.

• *Parent groups and disability agencies* can be lifelines for families who are learning the ropes of caring for a child with disability. Groups such as Parents Reaching Out (PRO) and the Association of Retarded Citizens (ARC) are settings where parents can come together and meet each other for educational, recreational, and peer support purposes. Parents of children with disability are dealing with exceptional circumstances, and as a result need additional community support from friends, family, and support groups.

Rural families often have to travel to find services suitable for their child. Often this means driving long distances to see a specialized doctor, to receive physical, speech or occupational therapy, to be measured for braces and wheelchairs, or to have certain medical conditions monitored and/or treated. In some rural locations, students must be bused to another school in their district to receive appropriate and accessible educational services. Small-town hospitals may not have the specialized staff familiar with critical conditions, and the child may have to be taken to a larger city during an emergency. This situation, like so many others when a disability is involved, can be an added burden on the family.

Cost

Unfortunately, the income level of a family can limit the quality of care a child receives in this country. Wealthy families have more choices, as they are able to go to prestigious clinics in search of the highest quality of care and treatment. Others have no alternative but to work with local professionals who may not have a depth of background regarding a certain disability. Doctor visits, surgeries, adaptive equipment, and accessible family vehicles can add up to enormous sums whether or not the family is eligible for assistance. If cost is not a factor, a family is able to fully examine and treat the needs of their child.

Where the budget is a concern, the needs of the child must be weighed alongside the needs of the entire family.

Assertiveness

The personality of a parent plays a significant role in obtaining necessary services for children with very special needs. Even when a service is mandated by law, for example the right to a free and appropriate education, parents must often fight for their rights through the multi-layered, user-unfriendly bureaucracy. We've all heard the phrase "the squeaky wheel gets the grease," and it certainly applies to getting services. This is an unfortunate situation, because all too often these parents have their hands full with daily care requirements. The last thing they need is to be writing to lawmakers or appealing to school administrators. Many of our current laws have resulted from this type of advocacy, and those parents deserve enormous gratitude. But we cannot forget the less active and vocal parents, who are equally concerned about their children, but lack the skills to get what they need.

Parents who are raising a child with disability have been dealing with "the system" throughout their child's life. Services may be available to an eligible child, but *only if* parents make the necessary effort of wading through the piles of forms and applications, will those services actually reach the child. Families are often familiar with agencies and government departments such as Medicaid/Medicare, Department of Vocational Rehabilitation, Social Security, hospitals and insurance carriers, and medical supply companies. They are also well-versed in activities such as IEP meetings (see Chapter 5: Special Services for Special Students), appeals procedures, orthopedic brace fittings, equipment ordering, disability vehicle licensing, and so on. Learning and climbing the ropes is no easy task, and even the most assertive and advocating parents can get burned out. Teachers may find themselves working with parents who have lost their trust and faith in the school system, having been forced to wage too many battles.

Teachers can be valuable allies to less assertive parents. If the parents are not acting on obtaining available services, consider the possibility that they are overwhelmed, shy, or ashamed of having the need in the first place. The shadow of disability's history of shame and hiding can undermine a family's belief that services are part of the child's rights. A teacher who is even minimally informed about support and referral services in the community can help lead the parents to someone who can help. Perhaps a parent will request the teacher's support in addressing the school board, or filling out applications for financial assistance in certain programs. Sometimes a parent will need help just brainstorming a solution to a problem situation. Parents often consult their medical doctors for advice and direction in matters concerning their child. In some cases, there are other opinions to be considered as well, and as their child's teacher, you may find them turning to you for help in answering questions. Your ability to explore the issues with them is in part dependent on your awareness of available services in your community.

An Important Part to Play

As you can see, there are many issues facing families who have a child with disability. You will probably come to see that most of these families have developed impressive character strengths in response to their unique situations. The demands upon them have been magnified, and their skills and abilities have grown in accordance. As you work with students who live with various disability, and their families, the most important criterion is to remember the depth of challenge they each carry. Remind yourself of the grief and frustration, the daily physical effort, the profound levels of acceptance that each family wears in its own personal way. Armed with this sort of compassion, you will be uniquely prepared in your position as teacher to support, listen to, fight for, laugh, and cry with the parents and siblings who need you. Disability is a human condition, and if we remember our humanity, our shared humanness, then our choices for words and action will be appropriate and appreciated.

Myths and Misconceptions

Parents of a child with disability are bitter and jealous of other children.

As with most myths, there are times when this might be true. However, it is much more likely to be a passing emotion than a deep-rooted, ongoing attitude. Parents of children with disability love their children as they are; they grow used to the extra requirements and enjoy their child's individuality. They can usually appreciate other children, both within and outside their family, without needing to compare them in unrealistic ways.

Parents of a child with disability would rather not talk about their child's situation.

If a child's disability is recent, his or her parents might indeed have a sensitivity about it during the adjustment period. Or, parents dealing with long-term disability may be tired of being asked over and over about their child's condition. On the other hand, once the family is used to the situation, it's usually not very different than talking about any child. Sometimes parents welcome the chance to talk to others about their child, since they may feel isolated or misunderstood. As a general rule, it's best to use sensitivity in approaching the subject of the child's disability.

People with disability often seem so well adjusted, like they've completely accepted it.

Very likely they have, but we don't want to make the mistake of thinking that disability is something one "gets over." Adjusting to a disability is a lifelong process that is regularly renewed by everyday experiences such as disrespectful treatment, inaccessibility, and recurring physical problems.

When someone becomes disabled, life is over.

While this idea may indeed feel true to some people with disability, it cannot be assumed to apply universally. Yes, depression and loneliness may accompany a disability, especially during the cycle of adjustment. Issues such as family support and community involvement play a part in whether an individual will feel their life is of little or no value. There are many, many people with disability leading happy, productive lives. In our work with students with disability, we have found that these young people, who have a deficiency of mental or physical abilities, so often have an excess of joy and innocence. They do not experience themselves as inferior, even though at times they feel left out or lonely. Disability may at times have the paradoxical effect of increasing one's appreciation for life. The danger with this misconception is that it has been established as a common role model for disability.

Aware of Our Words

Inappropriate: Judgmental attitudes, jumping to conclusions, telling someone what to do.

> "Just go away for the weekend and forget about all this."
> "You shouldn't be so impatient with her, she can't help being disabled."
> "Put him in the inclusion program—it will be good for him."
> "He is disabled." (Refers to his complete identity.)

Appropriate: Asking sensitive questions, being a good listener.

> "Is it hard adjusting to disability?"
> "What have you learned from having a child with disability?"
> "How do you feel about inclusion programs for your child?"
> "He has a disability." (Disability as one aspect of who he is, as a person.)

Ideas For Discussion

1. Personal Experience

Many students know or have known someone with a disability. They rarely have the opportunity to talk about their experiences or questions. Maybe they have stories of seeing someone in a store or in town, who exhibited a disability. If it is someone they know, what is their relationship and what types of things have they done together? If it is someone they saw, what made the impression? What questions do they have about that person's life? What have they learned about a particular disability as a result of knowing someone who lives with it? Have they ever seen this person mistreated, teased, or avoided? What did they feel in that situation? Did they do anything about it, or did they think about what they might have done?

2. Grief

Review the grief cycle with your class. There are many excellent materials available on this subject. Outline the stages of grief on a handout or chalkboard: anger, denial, bargaining, depression, acceptance. Ask students to think of a time when they lost something dear to them: the death of a loved one or pet, moving to a new town and school, not making a team or achieving a goal, having to live with a temporary disability from injury, etc. Any incident that they strongly did not want to happen is applicable. Can they recognize some of the stages in the feelings they had? Were some stages longer and harder than others? Did some of the stages come and go, such as anger or depression? What does acceptance feel like? Are there still times of sadness or frustration in remembering the loss? Are those feelings still intense, or have they subsided?

3. Life in a Family

Discuss the pros and cons of family life. What do your students enjoy about living with parents and siblings? What is difficult or annoying? In what ways do they take care of others? Do they have very young siblings who need physical care? Do they ever enjoy taking care of others, or is it always a bother? What are they looking forward to about being on their own? What will they miss? If they have siblings, what would it be like to be an only child? If the student is an only child, what would it be like to have siblings? Pets are usually physically dependent on their owners for food, exercise, bathing, etc. Discuss whether the students enjoy taking care of their pets. Why is it often so easy to give attention and care to an animal, who doesn't even participate with chores and responsibilities? Can our attitudes with pets help us with humans?

4. Life and Death Choices

Families caring for a child with a severe disability may find themselves in a situation of grave decision: how to handle a life-threatening illness. There are several questions that arise in this type of situation, that families are required to have on file with the school the child attends and with the family physician. One such medical order is called DNR, which stands for Do Not Resuscitate. In the event that the child stops breathing, or goes into cardiac arrest, emergency measures will not be taken to resuscitate. Oxygen may be provided, but no revival efforts will be administered when the physical system fails. A Living Will, or Advanced Directive, specifies what measures may or may not be taken by medical personnel in an emergency. The Living Will legally curtails the use of mechanical life support systems to keep a person alive, as in the case of coma or unconsciousness. This order allows individuals to avoid prolonging life in the event of an incapacitating injury or illness. The documents must be kept on file with the medical facility or school the child attends. These choices are very specific to each person or family.

After explaining each order, have the class discuss their personal choices, for themselves or for other family members. What if there was a sibling in the family who was entirely dependent? Would this affect their choices? What would some of the considerations be in making such a decision? Topics for discussion include: quality of life for the impaired individual; financial and emotional cost of ongoing care; religious and/or spiritual views and doctrines. What would be the hardest part about making this type of decision?

Lesson Plans

Photo Pages (grades 4–12)

See Lesson Plans in Chapter 2 for guidelines to using the photo pages for this chapter.

Guest Speaker: Parent or Sibling (grades 4–12)

Objective: To develop empathy and awareness in students through a personal encounter with an individual who lives with or cares for someone with a disability.
Timeframe: One to two class periods.
Steps:
1. Locate a person in your community who is a parent or sibling (young adult is preferable) of an individual with disability. Ask them if

they would be willing to speak to your class. You would like them to tell about their child's disability and some of the particulars about living with the child. Suggest some sample topics: How did their child come to have a disability? What kind of care does he or she need? Who provides the care? How do they travel? What types of activities do they enjoy together as a family? Have they experienced public attitudes towards their child? Perhaps the parent might bring along a sibling of the child with the disability, who could share a different point of view. Possible ways to find such a person include: ask students if they know someone who would be appropriate; inquire with other teachers or your special education staff; contact a local association or agency such as the Association for Retarded Citizens (ARC) or an independent living center. You will want to find someone who is able to speak well, and is receptive to the idea of educating young people about disability. It is recommended that you find someone through a reference who knows the individual personally, rather than just ask someone you don't know.

2. Spend a class period or part of one discussing some of the issues in this chapter, or one or more of the Ideas for Discussion. Help your students to imagine how their lives would be different if their sister or brother had a severe disability. Would they need a new car or van? Is their home accessible, could it be modified or would the family have to move? How would their parents' work schedules be affected?

3. Inform the students of the speaker who will be visiting your class. You might want to practice some sample questions in order to help the students feel comfortable with the issues. Students can give each other feedback on what is appropriate and sensitive and what is not. Encourage the students to think about any questions they might have before the visit.

4. Allow the speaker a full class period, even if he or she is finished earlier. Have the students write the guest a thank-you letter.

5. Continue discussion about family life with a child with disability. What impressed them about the speaker? What seemed most challenging about this family's life? What seemed most rewarding?

Creative Writing for Younger Students (grades 4–8)

Objective: To develop creative writing skills; to encourage students to consider another type of life experience; to have students identify qualities of character necessary in certain situations.

Timeframe: One to two class periods. (This can be a homework assignment that is discussed in class after completion.)

Steps:

1. Give the students the following instructions for their writing assignment:

Pretend you have a brother with a disability. Describe your brother. Then tell a story about what it's like to live with your brother. How do you play with him? How do you help your parents take care of him? What makes you angry or sad about having a brother who cannot do all the things you can do? Have the story include something that happens, for example your family takes a trip, or you take your brother to his school classroom.

2. Have the students share how they came up with the character for their brother. Was he based on someone they know or have seen? Have they ever had a similar experience that helped them write this story?

Creative Writing for Older Students (grades 9–12)

Objective: To develop creative writing skills; to encourage students to consider another type of life experience; to have students identify qualities of character necessary in certain situations.

Timeframe: One to two class periods. (This can be a homework assignment that is discussed in class after completion.)

Steps:

1. Following an activity or assignment which increases students' awareness of family issues involving a child with disability (Photo Pages, Ideas for Discussion, Guest Speaker), ask your students to write a poem about disability or a child with disability. The poem can be from any point of view: parent, sibling, self, observer, etc. The poem should address one or more of the challenges facing a person with a disability, or those caring for him/her. Some ideas for getting started:

feelings: Anger, frustration, joy, fear, peacefulness

thoughts: "Why me?" "If only....", "Why do people treat me like this?" "What I would like to change"

scenarios: A parent overloaded with taking care of a child with severe disability; the child's view and viewpoint while sitting in a classroom;

a family outing; a family cannot afford the new wheelchair; a mother has just been told her newborn baby has irreversible brain damage.

language: Using slang terms for disability in a poetic way to make a point about attitudes

2. Have the students type their poems. If they are comfortable, invite them to read aloud. Or, mount the poems on colored paper and post in a school hallway for others to read.

3. An alternate activity for performing the poems is to have the students make or bring in puppets who will read the poems. In this way, the students can remove themselves from being the primary performer, while still sharing the work with each other.

Sensitivity Training (grades 4–12)

Objective: To develop sensitivity in students for people with
   disability, and appreciation for challenges they face.
Timeframe: One day to one week.
Steps:
1. Choose a disability for the students to experience. Some suggestions include: wheelchair user, blindness, hearing impairment, or loss of one arm.

2. Obtain one or more wheelchairs from the special ed department, a physical therapy agency, or hospital rental supply. Have students take turns spending a day or a portion of a day using the wheelchair. They must understand that they are to do everything they need to do from the wheelchair. They should not get out of the chair to open a door or drink from a fountain. If they cannot do something from the chair, they need to ask for help. They should take the chair into the rest rooms as far as they can to use the toilet. If there is a handicapped stall, they must use it, and not a regular one. They may need to have someone carry their lunch tray, or their books.

3. If the students will be going to different classes with different teachers, give the students a note explaining the intent of the activity, asking for the other teachers' cooperation.

4. If the activity is blindness, have the student secure a full eye mask. This works best if two folded pieces of fabric are first laid on the eyes, then a scarf wrapped and tied at the back of the head. Be sure the student cannot see out the bottom edge.

5. For blindness training, have the student do it while in the classroom. Upon leaving the classroom, the student should have a companion to guide and assist. Be sure to stress safety precautions in this exercise. Pretending blindness can be very challenging for long periods of time, and the students can get a taste of it without reaching a point of extreme discomfort. It may work for the student to go to lunch in the cafeteria, or to the rest room, with assistance. The student must ask for help whenever needed, not take off the blindfold.

6. Hearing impairment: stuff cotton in ears or foam ear plugs, during lesson time. Loss of limb: tie one arm across the waist by wrapping a long strip of fabric around the waist. This can get very uncomfortable, so the student will need to take his or her arm out periodically. They might do this exercise during a specific part of the school day, for example lunch time.

7. Debrief the experiences by having a full class discussion, even if only some of the students participated in the actual activity. What was it like for them? Did they notice any attitudes from people? What was difficult about the activity? What was fun? Did they imagine what it would be like to really have a disability? What was frustrating? Did they have any new insights about the disability? Did they feel compassion for people who must live like that? Do any of them think they might see disability differently in the future, as a result of this practice?

Student Biography: Nathan

4.1: Nathan

When Nathan was born, his mother saw a beautiful, healthy, normal baby boy. After a while she began to notice that he didn't do things that other infants were doing, like rolling over or learning to sit up. At first, the doctors said everything was fine, she was just worrying. But when he was three, tests finally showed that she was right: Nathan had cerebral palsy, which caused his body not to develop or function properly. He cannot walk or talk, and he has limited use of his hands. Now, at age sixteen, Nathan loves life, is very alert, friendly, fun-loving, and knows exactly what people are doing and saying. He always wants to be included in activities, even if it's just watching, and sometimes he gets sad or angry that he can't do what other kids are doing.

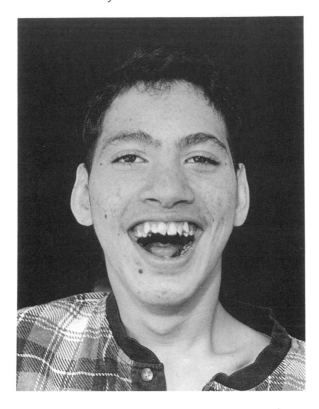

Figure 4.1 Nathan (photo by Ted Schooley).

Nathan lives in a Native American village, where they celebrate many occasions with dancing and feasts. When Nathan was younger, he had a very serious operation on his back, to keep his spine from curving. The operation was successful, and the people of the village held a very special feast to express their gratitude. Nathan's father and other men stood in front of the church all day and all night, and shot rifles into the air at the beginning and end of the feast time. The women cooked for several days, many different traditional foods. The entire community showed how thankful they were for Nathan's life. Having a severe disability is a challenge for the whole family. This beautiful support from the people in their village made Nathan's family know they were not alone.

Questions:

1. What other kinds of support from friends and neighbors could help Nathan's family take care of him?

? How do you think it would feel to be aware and have feelings, but have no voice to express yourself?

4.2: A Chance to Dance

Just like most teens, Nathan likes to dance, not an easy thing in a wheelchair. He needs to have someone hold him up, like the physical therapist in the picture. He's finally getting a chance to dance with his friend, Tracy. They don't really look like they're dancing because they stopped to have the picture taken. Doesn't it look like he's having fun?

Figure 4.2 A Chance to Dance (photo by Bill Davis).

You can see in the pictures that Nathan's arms and legs are very thin. This is because he doesn't use the muscles. His fingers and wrists stay stiff, which looks like it would be uncomfortable. If you tried to hold your wrist like that, it would hurt, but it doesn't hurt Nathan; that's just the way his body is. He has learned to use his hands and fingers with the small movements they can do. He can pick things up or press the keys of a computer, but cannot hold a pen to write.

The c.p. affects the mouth muscles Nathan would need to speak. He can grunt and make noises—very loud sometimes—and he tries very hard to say words. If a friend enters the classroom, Nathan gives a wordless holler to get his attention. Once the friend sees him, Nathan smiles and waves. Whoever said you needed words to be heard?

Questions:

1. What does it feel like if you make your hands and fingers very stiff and try to use them?

2. How much can someone communicate by making noises? Can the noises indicate different messages? How?

3. People with disabilities are often ignored. How would that feel? Why do you think Nathan makes noises to get attention?

4.3: The Stander

Part of Nathan's physical therapy program at school is to use a stander every day. He can actually stand without the stander, if someone supports him. The stander holds him upright, which helps his digestion and all his internal organs. However, it is very tiring after awhile, and Nathan signals to the therapist when he wants to get down. When someone is sitting down most of the time, it is very important for health reasons that he stand or lie down during part of the day.

Nathan usually uses an electric wheelchair that is controlled by a small knob on the armrest. He's had a lot of practice and is a very good driver, making sharp turns and maneuvering in tight places. The disadvantage of an electric chair is that it is very heavy and difficult to lift or load into a car. Nathan rides a school bus that has a wheelchair lift to get the chair in and out. Many cities now have buses with lifts, so that people like Nathan can use public transportation as well.

Figure 4.3 The Stander (photo by Bill Davis).

When Nathan first got his electric wheelchair he ran away from home in it. He was so thrilled with this new freedom, after being so many years in a chair that someone else had to push. Finally he could control his own movements instead of being dependent on others. The police found him and brought him home. His parents were quite angry because he had scared them by disappearing like that.

Questions:

1. How do you think your body would feel if you had to sit all day long? What would you want to do the most?

2. Was Nathan being foolish to run away? Give reasons for your answer.

3. Why do we need laws that require public buses to have wheelchair lifts?

4. How important is it for Nathan to have an electric wheelchair? If his family can't afford it, should the government pay?

4.4: The Big Ball

Nathan can't play baseball or basketball with his classmates. This big ball is the way he plays. He can roll it back and forth to another person. Even such a simple activity can be fun, and he enjoys it because it is one more thing he is able to do with other people.

Nathan loves life and is a very social person. Like most teenagers, much of his social life takes place in school. He rides through the halls and other students say "hi" to him. Nathan smiles, waves and nods his head. His smile is big and very happy. He is aware of everything going on around him, and gets a lot of enjoyment from being in the middle of activity. He'd like to be able to do a lot more than he does, especially with other kids, like going out to movies or parties, to have friends and outside activities.

Figure 4.4 The Big Ball (photo by Bill Davis).

When people ignore Nathan or shy away from him, he becomes frustrated and sad. With his computer voice he is able to tell his teachers and parents that it makes him feel sad to be rejected for his disability. At times, Nathan gets angry that he can't do things like other kids. It must be extremely difficult for him to have such full mental awareness and such limited physical ability.

Questions:

1. If you spent more time around people with disability, do you think it would help you feel more comfortable, or make you more uncomfortable?

2. Have you ever seen people shy away from a person in a wheelchair? Why are people uncomfortable around someone who is different?

3. If you were Nathan's parent, how might you have felt when you found out he had C.P.?

4.5: At the Computer

Nathan attends several general ed classes. He doesn't do homework and can't answer questions or take part in class discussions. He uses a computerized "voice" which is like a laptop computer that sits on a tray attached to his wheelchair, to talk to the teacher and other students. He loves being a member of these classes, such as Earth Science and Teen Issues. He also uses computers to do math and academics.

Nathan would like to have a job after graduating from high school. He might be able to manage a computer job, if it were very simple. There may come a time when Nathan lives separately from his family in a group home, but he will always need assistance with many things like getting dressed, bathed, and in and out of the wheelchair.

Nathan's family takes him out in the community a lot, to restaurants, movies, or shopping. When he's out, he loves getting noticed and greeted. He enjoys watching wrestling on television, and knows a lot about the N.W.O. He also likes girl-watching.

Like other people, Nathan has difficult emotional times. When he's not happy, he has very clear ways of expressing it. First, you can easily see it in his face when he's angry. He sometimes slams his bedroom door by pushing it with the wheelchair. He has even pulled posters off the wall. Being the teenager that he is, Nathan gets in trouble with his parents. They discipline him by cutting back on his privileges, like watching TV or going to school activities.

Figure 4.5 At the Computer (photo by Bill Davis).

Questions:

1. Does it seem possible for someone like Nathan to have a job? What would his boss need to learn, change or accept?

2. How is modern technology helping people like Nathan to live fuller lives?

3. Why might Nathan get so angry at times? Would you, if you were in his situation?

4. If Nathan can do math, what does that tell you about his mental ability?

Chapter 5

SPECIAL SERVICES FOR SPECIAL STUDENTS

Within the public school system of our country, special education is like a world unto itself. Born out of legislation mandating public schooling for all children regardless of disability, special education has grown into a comprehensive department which stands side by side with, and sometimes overlaps, general education programs. Special education addresses the individual needs of students whose disabilities adversely affect their learning needs. Most of the components of special education are dictated by federal and state laws. Every state will vary to some degree in how the program is administered; some of the components will be very similar to other states or districts, and others very different. Rather than confuse the reader with all the possibilities, this chapter presents a basic overview of the special education process, such as who is eligible and what services are provided. Having this type of fundamental information can help teachers know where to look for help for a student, and understand what services might accompany a student with disability in the classroom.

Determination of Services

How a child enters the special ed department can happen in a number of ways. If a disability has been present and diagnosed from birth or early infancy, that child will probably have been receiving intervention services prior to school age. These children come into the school system with a history of information on abilities, limitations, and special needs, making them immediately eligible for special education enrollment through which an appropriate program can be designed.

Other children begin school with no prior indication of disability. Cognitive, hearing, or visual impairments are examples of disabilities that often remain undetected in early years living at home. Once the child is in a classroom setting, a new set of behaviors is expected, which can reveal an inability to perform, pay attention, or communicate. It is very common for learning disability to become apparent when students begin reading or doing math. In these situations, the teacher will notice that a student is having difficulty in some area of performance or behavior. The child is referred for assessment, and a team meets to try to identify the problems and possible solutions. Interventions and strategies for maintaining a general education placement are usually the first course of action, but sometimes are not adequate. The next step is a complete evaluation to determine the possibility of special education placement. Only by examining the student's skill level in several areas of functioning can an appropriate plan be developed. Special education services require that the student have a disability that falls within one of the qualifying conditions. If the school is not able to provide the necessary services, then the district is responsible to finance a private program for the student, either at home or in another institution.

Section 504

A term that is frequently used in special ed departments refers to a part of the Rehabilitation Act of 1973. Section 504 was the first law to address discrimination against people with disability, by requiring physical accessibility in federal buildings and institutions, and in any institutions receiving federal moneys. Since public schools are partially supported by federal aid, they are subject to this ruling. Section 504 applies to students who need physical accommodation to attend school. With proper accommodation, these students are capable of academic learning with their peers, and do not require special education services. An example would be a student who uses a wheelchair for an orthopedic impairment, while having full mental capacity. Accommodations include ramps to classes, auditorium, cafeteria, accessible bathrooms; desks or tables fitted for a wheelchair; a laptop computer; and any other adaptation needed for the student to equally access his or her educational opportunities. Students who have visual or hearing loss might also be recipients of 504 services. Whereas special education services are required by, and funded by, the federal government, provision of 504 services falls to the individual state and school district.

The Individualized Education Plan

Every public education teacher is familiar with the term IEP, which stands for the Individualized Education Plan which is the backbone of special education services. The purpose of the plan is to ensure that every student gets the maximum benefit of the educational system, by receiving personal assessment, planning, and review. An IEP is required for every student receiving special education services. The plan determines what services are needed for students to receive educations equal to those of their peers without disability. An IEP is developed when a student enters special education, and is reviewed annually. A complete reassessment is required every three years.

Decisions regarding a student's educational options are not made by a single person, but by a well-balanced team of professionals that has the ability to consider the full picture of what the child needs. Team members vary, depending on the exact nature of the impairment. The team is commonly made up of some of the following: the student's parents (and sometimes the student), a physician, a physical therapist, an occupational therapist, a speech pathologist, general and special education teachers, and the educational diagnostician or psychologist/psychiatrist. The educational diagnostician is often the professional who administers and interprets the evaluation tests. Most general education teachers will participate on a student's multidisciplinary team from time to time.

Once a student is determined to be eligible for services, the team must decide: full inclusion, partial inclusion, or no inclusion? The law specifies inclusion as much as is appropriate, considering that each student has individual needs which influence the answer. Some students need very specialized instruction, more than could be expected of a general education teacher already responsible for a full class. Those students might spend part of the day in a general ed setting, and part of the day with therapists, specialized teachers, or aides. Other students with disability might function very well in a full-time general education setting, if provided with certain modifications or part-time aides.

Each school district creates its own IEP form, using fairly standard areas of documentation. The form is usually several pages in length, and requests information such as student identification, teacher and parent observations, opportunities for general education program participation, special education and related services, least restrictive educational environment, classroom modifications, graduation standards, physical education program, disciplinary strategies, and any other specific issues for the student.

Related Services

Along with the special education teacher, the special education department includes a group of professional therapists who provide related services to students with disability. The services are delivered in both general education and special education classrooms, and must be educationally necessary for the completion of IEP objectives. Becoming familiar with related staff roles and services gives teachers an idea of where to look for help when a student is exhibiting particular problems.

Occupational Therapy

Occupational therapy, also referred to as O.T., focuses on the student's ability in the areas of hand skills, self-feeding skills, self-care and grooming, social skills, and play/leisure skills. For young adults approaching graduation, occupational therapy works within the same areas, focusing also on employment skills, crafts, and living (home) skills. The occupational therapist develops strategies and creative activities to enhance the student's performance and ability.

Physical Therapy

Physical therapists (P.T.) work to evaluate and improve a person's physical ability, such as joint motion, muscle strength, functional ability, muscle tone and reflexes. When needed, they assess the appearance and stability of a student's walking, and determine the need and use of braces or artificial limbs. Also within the range of P.T. is heart and lung function, sensation and perception, and how well the individual performs daily living activities. The physical therapist often works with students in the self-contained classroom, on padded mats or parallel bars. Sometimes therapy is provided in the gym, or in a regular classroom.

Speech Therapy

Speech therapy is also referred to as speech-language pathology, and it applies to the prevention or improvement of problems in the field of speech, cognition, swallowing, articulation, voice, verbal or written language, or any other aspect of communication that has to do with talking. Students with speech disorders may leave the classroom to receive individual therapy from the speech therapist during the school day.

Audiology Services

Audiology services are provided to students with hearing impairment. Audiologists determine the range, nature and degree of the hearing loss. They may work with students on language skills, auditory training, speech, and reading. The audiologist creates programs for prevention of hearing loss, as well as counseling students with hearing disability. The audiology department, along with the student's physician, determines if the student needs hearing aids, and which type is most beneficial.

Psychological Services

Psychological services are provided by the school psychologist, and also by outside professionals who might be working privately with the student, or called upon for specific evaluations. Psychologists administer evaluation tests, and make recommendations for the planning of school programs. Students with disability may receive counseling services from the psychologist, to help them deal with issues related to social adjustment.

Social Work Services

School social workers provide a range of services, some of which apply to the student with disability. They are responsible for understanding the student's social and developmental history, and how it might affect school performance. Social workers provide counseling for the student on personal issues, family issues, school situations, academic choices, and social issues. For the student with severe disability, the social worker can offer assistance to the parents, informing them of various community services or financial aid options.

Skilled Nursing

Skilled nursing is a specialized sector of nursing that works specifically with the medically fragile student. Trained for emergency situations that may arise for the child with severe disability, their services include such procedures as blood-sugar monitoring, oxygen monitoring, and suctioning of airways. Any student who has impaired lung capacity or a tendency to have seizures may need the services of a skilled nurse from time to time. Often the skilled nurses will work in self-contained classrooms, or general education classrooms that include a student with severe disability.

Mobility and Orientation

This category of service was developed to help individuals whose sight and hearing impairments make mobility difficult. The mobility and orientation therapist works with these students to develop hearing skills and sensation of body movements, in order to increase their ability to negotiate school hallways, doors, curbs, stairways, etc. The student with very low vision can learn to use a guide cane, or to rely on sound for sensing one's location in the environment. Someone with hearing loss needs to be able to interpret signs that usually come from sound, such as a horn honking, or someone speaking. These skills will help the student function more independently and safely.

Types of Disability

Categories of disability did not always exist. In past centuries, disabilities were referred to in more general terms. Lame, crippled, dumb, moron, crazy, half-wit: these were the terms used to describe an individual's condition. There was no need for clinical classifications until there were services that required eligibility standards. As the idea developed that people with disability were entitled to particular types of help, rather than just to charity, it became the responsibility of the government to provide assistance to those who could not provide for themselves. Those who were entitled to receive help became identified by categories which have become more and more refined over the years.

The following definitions, outlined by IDEA-B, are only one way that disabilities can be classified. They could also be separated into mental and physical groupings, or mild/ moderate/ severe. A recent grouping refers to "low incidence" and "high incidence" disabilities. One important thing to remember when considering categories of disability is how quickly they change. As legislation continues to refine and expand special education services, teachers will be seeing new terms, titles, and categories for classifying students with disability. The following list is offered as a current index of qualifying disabilities, as specified by the Individuals with Disabilities Education Act, which (even when outdated) gives an indication of the various components of disability.

Intellectually Disabled

Other terms: Mentally retarded (m.r.), mentally handicapped, developmentally delayed (d.d.–used incorrectly for this category; see Developmentally Delayed below), cognitively impaired, cognitively handicapped or delayed, intellectually impaired (i.i.).

Intellectually disabled means that the child has significantly sub-average intellectual functioning. The largest number of students receiving special education services falls within this category. Originally, the basis for determination of intellectual impairment was the IQ test. However, many students of minority heritage were found to be mentally impaired according to the test as well as in academic performance. Ironically, they were perfectly capable of all aspects of life outside school (interpersonal communication, personal care, crossing streets, riding buses, etc.). The students' cultural orientation was different from that of the school system and testing model. This situation revealed a cultural bias in the test itself, and, as a result, two additional criteria were added to the basic requirement of IQ scoring.

1. The student must have a sub-average IQ score;

2. There must be a deficit in adaptive behavior, that is, how the student functions in daily life skills;

3. The student must exhibit a significant academic delay or deficit.

Within the category of intellectually disabled, there are various degrees of severity, resulting in different levels of need and ability. Mild mental retardation is the most common level, accounting for approximately 80% of people with this disability. As the level of intellectual disability increases, it is often accompanied by some form of physical limitation. The levels are as follows:

• *Mild: IQ of 50 to 70:* Individuals with this degree of intelligence often have good verbal skills. They can commonly be well-integrated into a general education classroom, with minimal individualized assistance and modification of curriculum. Learning requires simplified and repeated instructions, and may still take additional time. Many students with mild mental retardation will be capable of employment after graduating; semi-independent living is possible in a group home or supported living program. They are able to relate to peers, and understand when someone is making fun of their differences. Early identification and intervention for individuals with mental retardation can increase their development and eventual independence.

• *Moderate: IQ of 35 to 49:* Moderate mental retardation impairs all aspects of cognitive functioning. Students with moderate mental retardation may be able to learn minimal reading skills. In the classroom, these students need a modified curriculum. Such impairment makes it difficult to retain information, and students will need to be instructed many times before learning a task. They will not always be in sync with what is taking place around them, and because of reduced awareness of social cues from peers, may have difficulty with relationships.

• *Severe: IQ of 20 to 34:* Severe mental retardation is almost always evident at an early age. Communication with a student of this level can be frustrating and difficult, even using the simplest instructions. They will probably have trouble expressing their needs, and the teacher may find it difficult to understand the communication. It is not unusual to get a "yes" response to opposite questions, for example: "Do you want to go to the store?" and, "Do you want to stay home?" These students are also unaware of social norms, and may display inappropriate behaviors, such as performing personal body functions in public. Students with this level of impairment can be easily frustrated by waiting as well; like a very young child, they have no concept of time, and will want something immediately that is not due for several hours. In a general education classroom, the student with severe mental retardation will most likely have an accompanying aide.

• *Profound: IQ of 20 or below:* Students with IQs below 20 will be dependent on others for all aspects of care. They will not have verbal skills, and communication is usually limited to very simple body language. A personal aide should be assigned for this type of student in inclusion settings. However, these students can and do benefit from participating in the general education class. They receive stimulation and enjoyment from joining in or observing simple activities. Care should always be taken not to overstimulate the student with profound mental retardation.

In an inclusion classroom setting, teachers must be aware that the intellectually impaired student will not be picking up the same social cues as the other students. Jokes, teasing, peer relationships, and body language may be wrongly or incompletely interpreted. Certain basic skills may or may not be achievable, depending on the individual. It is not uncommon for social and personal functioning to improve as the child grows into maturity.

Hearing Impaired (including Deafness)

Other terms: hard of hearing, hearing disabled, communication disordered (used incorrectly for this category), dumb.

Hearing impaired refers to the child who has some degree of hearing loss, from mild to full deafness, but severe enough to adversely affect educational performance. Hearing impairments affect one out of every 50 school children. The impairment can be permanent and complete; it can also be fluctuating, where the severity changes under certain circumstances. Some hearing impairments are unilateral, meaning that only one ear is affected. Total deafness is rare and is usually present from birth. Partial deafness is most commonly the result of an ear disease or injury. Extremely loud noises can damage the hearing mechanism, as can having a foreign object lodged in the ear canal.

A student with this disability may exhibit signs of difficulty following classroom interactions and activities, requiring assistance and attention in certain areas of instruction. There may also be a limited vocabulary. Teachers can usually adapt a classroom environment to accommodate a student with severe hearing loss or deafness, without too much difficulty. The speech and language therapist is able to provide assistance and suggestions for improving communication potential between the student and the rest of the class.

Visually Impaired

Other terms: Blind, legally blind, visually handicapped/disabled, visual disorder.

This term defines students who have an impairment of vision which is significant enough, even with correction, to adversely affect educational performance. Children who are partially seeing as well as fully blind are included in this definition. Vision loss may affect one or both eyes, with partial or complete blindness. An inability to see may develop slowly or suddenly; it can be present from birth or result from injury or disease. The most common forms of visual disorders are due to simple errors of how the light rays enter and are processed in the eye. Glasses can almost always correct the blurring of vision from this type of problem. However, there are many visual impairments that cannot be corrected with lenses.

Students who have visual disability, but are fully functioning in cognitive abilities, may not need to be enrolled in a special education program. If the problem is solely physical, the school is required by Section 504 to provide accommodations for the student such as Braille equipment, large print materials, or allowing the use of audio taping in class.

Deaf/Blind

This category combines aspects of the two preceding ones. It refers to the student who exhibits both hearing and visual impairments which adversely affect educational performance. To fall under this category, the combination of impairments must produce significant communication, developmental, and educational needs that cannot be met by services which are usually provided for either deaf children or blind children.

The combination of deafness and blindness creates a unique communication challenge, in that the conscious intellect of the individual cannot be reached either by sound or sight. People who are blind can learn communication skills through hearing and language. When deaf, they learn visually. But when both senses are affected, it creates an extreme situation of separation from others, even though they may have perfectly unimpaired intelligence. A student with this disability will need to be attended by a mobility and orientation therapist in a general education setting. Helen Keller is the most well-known person who had this combination of disabilities. The moving story of her childhood breakthrough was made famous in the play *The Miracle Worker* by William Gibson. The only way she was able to be reached was through touch; Helen's teacher would make hand signs while holding Helen's hand on her own. Eventually Helen was able to understand that the signs related to objects and ideas.

Speech-Language Impaired

Other terms: Speech impairment/disability or handicap, language impairment/disability or handicap, speech or language disorder, communication disorder.

This category refers to students who have a disorder such as stuttering, poor articulation, language impairment, or voice impairment, which adversely affects their educational performance. Although classified jointly, there is a notable difference between a language disorder and a speech disorder. Language refers to the mental process of understanding spoken or written words. Speech has to do with the physical ability (mouth, tongue, vocal cords) to form and pronounce words. Both speech and language impairments can affect learning skills and a student's classroom adjustment. This type of condition can also be a contributing factor to learning disability, which is discussed below.

In terms of classroom situations, speech impairment can be very difficult for a teacher to understand, especially at first. However, comprehending unusual speech patterns becomes easier over time. Understanding grows if the listener takes the time to ask the speaker to repeat and repeat and repeat! For a period, this will be frustrating, and even seem impossible. But eventually, the speech becomes more familiar to the listener. Learning to communicate with an individual with serious speech impairment is a joint effort, and requires much patience.

Seriously Emotionally Disturbed

Other terms: Serious emotional disturbance, SED, behaviorally different/challenged, emotionally disordered/disturbed, mentally ill.

This classification includes any condition which exhibits one or more of the following characteristics over an extended period of time, and to a marked degree:

• an inability to learn, which cannot be explained by intellectual, sensory, or other health factors;

• an inability to develop or maintain satisfactory interpersonal relationships with peers and teachers;

• inappropriate types of behavior or feelings under normal circumstances;

• a general, pervasive mood of unhappiness or depression;

• a tendency to develop physical symptoms or fears associated with personal or school problems.

Emotional disturbance covers a wide range of psychological difficulties. The problems may be due to dysfunctional family life, including abuse and neglect, or to psychiatric illness which may or may not be genetic. Feelings of anxiety and depression are usually predominant in these individuals.

Mental illness is a general term that describes any form of psychiatric disorder. Severe psychological disorders are usually caused by biochemical dysfunction in the brain, and affect one's ability to communicate or function. One example of this type of disorder is schizophrenia. Less disturbing psychological conditions may result from poorly functioning family systems. A common form of less severe mental illness is a manic/depressive condition. Many psychiatric disorders respond well to medications.

Attention deficit disorder (ADD) and attention deficit hyperactivity disorder (ADHD) are included in this definition only when behavior is the primary symptom, and when the behavior problem is severe enough to adversely affect educational performance. However, ADD and ADHD manifest in a number of different ways, which makes placement an individual situation for each student. In the following section, these disorders are discussed more fully.

Many variations of emotional and behavioral disturbance can fall into this category. Hyperactivity is generally a milder form of behavioral problems which teachers will regularly see in their classrooms. Students exhibiting the more serious emotional or behavioral problems will usually be placed in special behavior disorder classes (B.D.), alternative schools, or psychiatric institutions.

Orthopedically Impaired

Other terms: multiply impaired (m.i.), multiply handicapped.

Orthopedically impaired refers to those individuals who have impairment of their structural, or skeletal, form severe enough to adversely affect performance in school. The category of orthopedic impairment is sometimes accompanied by one or more other conditions that will describe the child as "multiply impaired."

Orthopedic disability can be present from birth, or can be caused by disease or genetic developments as the individual matures. One example of this occurrence is scoliosis, a curvature of the spine which, when extreme, can develop into a hunchback condition. Some of the more familiar orthopedic impairments include: dwarfism, clubfoot, malformed, shortened, or missing limbs. These students will commonly use leg or arm braces, body braces, or wheelchairs. If cognitive functioning is not affected, many are able to perform academically in a general education curriculum. Special seating, desk arrangements, ramps, and assistive equipment all must be furnished as required by Section 504. Some of these students will also receive services such as physical therapy, occupational therapy, or speech therapy. The services are not provided as medical treatments, but only when they will enable the student to participate in a full day of school.

Traumatic Brain Injury

Other terms: head injury, brain damage, TBI.

This term defines an injury to the brain caused by external physical force or by an internal occurrence such as a stroke or aneurysm. This type of injury can cause total or partial disability in areas of memory, reasoning, language, speech, or mobility. The injury can affect just one area, or several, thereby creating a more complex condition, including epileptic seizures. Cerebral palsy is sometimes the result of traumatic brain injury.

Traumatic brain injuries range from mild to severe. One person may function perfectly well in all other areas, but have a serious memory problem, short-term or long-term. Another individual may lose the ability to put thoughts into words and sentences. Another may no longer be able to move his or her limbs, requiring total care. A common emotional response to brain injury is depression.

This can be a difficult disability to work with, as the effects of the injury are not necessarily consistent or apparent. Unlike mental retardation, brain injury can affect one area of function to an extreme, while the rest of the individual's abilities are quite normal or even above average.

Autism

Other terms: idiot/autistic savant (incorrect or only applicable to specific cases).

Autism means a developmental disability significantly affecting the verbal communication and social interaction of the child, generally before the age of three. Typical characteristics of autism include:

• irregularities in communication: eye contact may be difficult or impossible for the child, speech may be incoherent, mental awareness is inconsistent;

• repetitive activities and movements, such as rocking or rhythmic hand or head movements;

• resistance to changes in the environment or in daily routine, which are often very upsetting to the individual;

• unusual responses and sensitivity to noises, touch, or visual stimulus.

Autism is a rare condition, occurring in about three out of every ten thousand children. Nearly three times more boys than girls are affected, and it seems to have a more frequent occurrence in the higher social classes. Some children with autism are incapable of communication and social interaction, while others maintain partial function or intermittent abilities. The term "idiot savant," or more recently "autistic savant," refers to those individuals with autism who exhibit extraordinary abilities in certain areas, such as memory, math, or music. For example, there are people who can memorize entire telephone books or dictionaries, or mentally calculate complicated formulas instantly. This manifestation of the disability is a rare occurrence within the autistic population, approximately ten percent.

Team work is important for the child with autism, in order to ensure reaching his or her full potential. Depending on the behaviors of the student with autism, a one-on-one aide is assigned, to help control disruptive behaviors and support participation in general activities. Over time, some individuals with autism can learn self-control, although it usually requires great effort.

Other Health Impaired

Other terms: medically fragile, medically involved, or the specific health problem of the individual child will be referred to.

This category applies to children whose strength or alertness is limited, owing to a health problem which adversely affects their ability to perform in school. Common examples include: heart conditions, tuberculosis, rheumatic fever, asthma, sickle-cell anemia, hemophilia, epilepsy, leukemia, or diabetes. Some conditions cause a chronic level of fatigue for the child, while others will bring on periodic attacks of illness, interrupting school attendance or the child's ability to complete assignments. Often the student's specialized educational program must address decreased attendance, and incorporate home or hospital schoolwork as part of the plan.

Asthma, which causes difficulty inhaling oxygen, is the most common condition found in this category, affecting ten to fifteen percent of the general population. Diabetes is another prevalent condition that exhibits dangerous symptoms when blood sugar and insulin levels are out of balance. In either case, teachers of these types of students should receive information from the nursing staff regarding symptoms, medications, side effects, and emergency responses. Foresight and preparation allow teachers to feel more confident in handling any emergencies that arise, and the student will feel safer knowing that someone is well-informed.

Developmentally Delayed

Other terms: Developmental disability (d.d.). According to the specific area of development affected, any number of terms will be applied to a child within this category.

A developmental delay is applicable to children of ages three to eight, who are in need of special education services because of a significant delay or deficit in one or more of the following areas of development: cognitive, physical/ motor, language, social/ emotional, self-help, vision, or hearing.

The term developmental delay indicates the period of time when a child's mental and physical abilities are maturing within a particular range. Sometimes this type of delay is temporary, and in time the child will catch up with his or her peers. More often, children in this category remain deficient in one or more areas as they grow older, at which point the classification becomes intellectual impairment. Students within this category are usually in their first years of elementary school.

Specific Learning Disabled

Other terms: Dyslexic, learning disabled (l.d.).

A child who has learning disability has a disorder in one or more of the basic psychological processes involved in understanding or in using language, either spoken or written. These students usually have average intelligence, but achievement in one or more academic areas is significantly below average. The impairment may manifest in an inability to listen, think, speak, read, write, spell, or perform mathematical calculations. Dyslexic is a term often used incorrectly to apply to any reading disability. This condition refers very specifically to the inability to connect verbal sounds with visual letters.

Learning disability has reached notable proportions within our school populations. There are various theories as to the cause of the increase, foremost among them the idea that testing systems have been refined to allow more comprehensive diagnosis of learning disability, even in less obvious forms. In past decades, only the students with the most severe disability were identified and given the extra help they needed. Many other students were unwittingly called stupid or lazy, when their real trouble was one of physiological origin. Today, if a student exhibits difficulty in learning, testing for a learning disability is almost always the first step. These students are usually able to perform adequately within a general education class, receiving additional sup port from special education staff or remedial reading and math programs.

Attention Deficit Disorders

Not every student with ADD or ADHD will receive special education services. There are basically four options for determining eligibility and placement.

1. If behavior is the primary problem, the student will fall into the category for Seriously Emotionally Disturbed, which also covers behavioral difficulties.

2. If academic performance is the primary problem, with little or no behavior symptoms, the placement will be in the Specific Learning Disabled category.

3. If the student requires medication, and there is a medical diagnosis regarding reduced alertness, vitality or strength, the student may receive services under Other Health Impairments.

4. If the student does not qualify for any of the above placements, he or she will not receive special education services.

How each child is categorized depends completely on the particular IEP committee. A child could move to another district or state and be placed under a different category for the same symptoms. Many parents are opposed to labeling their child as Seriously Emotionally Disturbed, and may even refuse services if that is the identified category. Some students, who truly need additional help in learning, will end up falling through the cracks of the system. In those cases, general ed teachers find themselves providing whatever help they can to supplement the student's performance.

Attention deficit disorder (ADD) refers to inability to stay focused. Attention deficit hyperactivity disorder (ADHD) is a lack of attention accompanied by hyperactivity. Many children are loosely referred to as hyperactive, without the full disorder being identified. Hyperactivity may affect as many as five to ten percent of children in the United States, and is four to five times more common in boys than in girls. There are many different explanations for the growing numbers of hyperactive children in recent decades. Some believe that the numbers reflect advanced diagnosis testing, which is able to detect the condition in less extreme forms. Others attribute the disorders to increased television viewing, computer and video games, processed foods, food dyes and additives, medicinal drug increases (antibiotics), less quality family time, and all the other variables of modern life. One theory proposes that hyperactive children, especially those who are clumsy, may have a subtle form of "minimal" brain damage. Studies have examined the similarities between patterns of hyperactivity and those of manic-depressive conditions. Currently there is no conclusive proof, despite much supporting evidence, for any of these theories.

The main feature of hyperactivity is continual movement, which is often worse in the classroom or group setting, due to the increased stimulation of numbers of people. Hyperactive children are always on the go, full of energy, fidgety, and seem to sleep less than their peers. They tend to be impulsive and reckless, with little or no sense of danger, and are usually irritable, emotionally immature, and aggressive. Their attention span is short and, as a result, they do not conform to an orderly school routine. Those who are diagnosed can be treated with stimulant drugs such as Ritalin, which have a paradoxical calming effect on children. Diets that avoid certain artificial food colorings, additives, and refined sugars are often promoted, but research has shown that these diets benefit very few children. In many cases, hyperactivity disappears completely at puberty. In others, the over-activity subsides, only to be replaced by sluggishness, depression, and moodiness. For young people who are able to navigate the rough waters of adolescence, hyperactivity rarely continues into adult life.

Specialized Discipline

General ed teachers may discover that the issue of school discipline is also affected by law. IDEA-B outlines specific regulations governing disciplinary actions for the student with disability. If the student's behavior is *not* a manifestation of the disability, the student may be disciplined in the same manner as his or her peers without disability. If the behavior *is* a manifestation of the disability, then the student is treated differently. In other words, the law makes provision for students whose disability causes inappropriate behaviors. The student may not be expelled if the offense is related to the disability. The offense must be addressed without forfeiting the student's educational needs, for example by placement in an alternative school or setting. This ruling recognizes that students with certain disabilities do not need punishment, incarceration, or removal. They need a more appropriate setting to control the problem behaviors, and, more importantly, they need to continue receiving as full an education as possible.

Invisible Disability

Whether a disability is visible or invisible is of little concern to school administrators who are required to provide an appropriate education, regardless of appearance. However, such a distinction will have a notable difference in the way a child or adult exhibiting disability is treated by others. Previous chapters have examined how people with visible disability are mistreated and avoided. What about those with invisible conditions that affect behavior, thought patterns, speech, or hearing? Negative reactions can be even stronger, because there is no obvious explanation to excuse an unusual behavior.

When a person behaves outside the normal social standards, he or she is often judged as stupid, lazy, or rude. The reactions from others can be angry, impatient, and insulting. Recall the story that opens Chapter 1, about a young man named Tony. The cashier at the grocery store gets angry when Tony cannot count his money quickly. The busy clerk assumes the boy is wasting time, fooling around, when actually he is trying very hard to accomplish the task at hand. Tony is a good example of the difficulties of living with an invisible disability. He meets with those humiliating situations constantly. He looks great on the outside, but his brain doesn't function so great on the inside. He looks like a healthy teenager, but it takes him longer to do things. People don't understand, and so they treat him as they would any other young man on the checkout line.

Invisible disability includes any condition that affects a person's ability to function or communicate, but doesn't show externally. Some examples include mild mental retardation, deafness, health impairments that cause excessive fatigue or weakness, chronic pain, and mental illness. Invisible disability has its own set of challenges. In some ways, life may be easier for the individual when the disability is hidden. There are many situations where the person can avoid uncomfortable public responses: staring, insensitive questions, assumptions, etc. But in other ways it is harder, because the person often has to repeatedly inform others, in order not to be misunderstood. No one wants to wear a sign saying, "Make these allowances for me because I have a disability that you can't see." Having an invisible disability still leaves one open to ridicule, mistreatment, and impatience.

In our mid-size town, the Association of Retarded Citizens does an outstanding job helping people with cognitive disability integrate into the community through appropriate employment and living situations. One man in their program was working as a bus person in a local restaurant. We overheard a customer complaining that he was too slow and that he talked too much. We explained that he was impaired mentally, and was actually functioning exceptionally well for his level of development. Her whole attitude changed immediately! Once she understood that his abilities were limited, she was very willing to see his behaviors as positive and valuable. She made an effort to befriend him, telling us how wonderful it was that he could be an active member of the community.

Think of situations where someone acted in a strange way towards you. Maybe you thought that person was rude, or even frightening. Not understanding the behavior, maybe you judged the individual as "weird." Think again. Maybe that person had a head injury, mental illness, or a communication disorder that prevented full understanding of what was happening. There are many people on this planet who have invisible disability. Remembering this information may increase tolerance for those who are different with no apparent reason. The next time you are confronted with a person who seems unreasonably rude or slow to comprehend, remind yourself that it may be an invisible disability, and your patience in the situation will be a welcome gift for everyone involved.

Myths and Misconceptions

Autism is a result of neglect.

Autism is an unusual disability that has been well researched for many years. There is no evidence that it occurs only in children whose families do not pay attention to them.

All hyperactive children need drug therapy.

While Ritalin and other prescription medicines are helpful, even life changing, for some children, there remain a number of children who do not respond favorably to the use of drugs. Many parents are also concerned about possible long-term side effects of the treatment, and prefer to seek alternative methods of controlling behaviors.

Hyperactive children are neglected by their parents.

There are many informal theories about the root causes of hyperactivity, and its phenomenal increase in the past few decades. Once again, there are no conclusive answers, and the fact that hyperactivity affects children from many different home situations seems to dispute such catch-all solutions such as neglect or diet.

Children who act like they don't understand the teacher are just trying to get attention from their classmates.

Many times the student who plays "stupid" or always gives a comical answer, is actually at a loss to perform as required. In order to cover up for the inadequacies of a learning disability, the student will joke and find other ways to avoid giving the wrong answer, which would reveal his or her lack of comprehension.

"All students with a visual impairment need enlarged type and special seating."

Visual impairments can affect a student's sight in various ways. For example, a student who has decreased peripheral sight can see fine whatever is directly in front of the line of sight, without special adaptation.

If someone is hard of hearing, we must talk louder and slower.

If someone has a mental impairment, we must talk louder and slower.

If someone has a hearing loss, they don't understand very well.

All of these assumptions are incorrect! Some people who are hard of hearing can read lips so well that the speaker whispers and can still be understood. Some can hear better if there is less background noise and distraction. People with mental impairment may indeed appreciate a slower rate of speech, but there is probably nothing wrong with their hearing. They do not need to be shouted at! If someone cannot hear well, and asks you several times to repeat yourself, it does not indicate that they don't understand, just that they didn't hear you. Once they can hear the words, they will probably have no problem with the content.

Aware of Our Words and Actions

Inappropriate:
• Slang terms for disabilities, such as idiot, gimp, crip, retardo, retard, four-eyes, hyper, spazz.
• Standing up while talking to a person in a wheel chair, who needs to tip his or her head back in order to look at you.
• Patting on the head a person in a wheelchair, because of his or her low height, rather than on the back or shoulder.
• "She is an invalid."
The word *invalid* means *not valid*. It is appropriate to use this word in reference to things like licenses, permits, and competitions. It is very insulting to use this term for a person. Physical disability does not negate the basic value and worth of a human being.

Appropriate:	• "She has a disability and is completely dependent."
	• Using correct terms for a person's disability, even if it seems very technical.
	• Finding a chair or squatting next to a person in a wheelchair, in order to have a conversation at eye level.

Ideas For Discussion

1. The Use of Categories

After a presentation to your class about the concept of special education in general, and IDEA-B in specific, discuss the various categories and why it might have become necessary to develop them. Why is it important that students are determined to be eligible or not? Couldn't we just provide help for students on an as-needed basis? How is the school system affected by the inclusion of special education students? How does being categorized help the students with disability? Imagine the days before special education, when a student with any kind of disability came to school. What kind of situations might have led to the development of special education, as a concept and as a reality? How might this system have originated?

2. School Performance

Each of the IDEA-B definitions includes the phrase "and adversely affects the child's educational performance." Why is this specifically added to each definition? What does educational performance refer to: physical, emotional, social, mental/cognitive, etc.? In each area of performance, how might the school need to make adaptations for a particular student? Do these categories have a different purpose than a medical diagnosis? How would a medical diagnosis be useful in classifying a student by educational definitions? Have the class brainstorm disabilities that would not adversely affect a child's school performance. What do those disabilities have in common? Are there some disabilities that do not need special education services? What are some examples?

3. Intelligence Quotient

Discuss the concept of IQ testing, how it is calculated and the purposes it serves. Is intelligence something connected only to grades and school? Discuss how intelligence affects different areas of competency, such as school performance, creative thinking, verbal and conceptual abilities, problem-solving, etc. Why does a lower IQ mean that someone will be incapable of ever developing certain mental abilities? Does intelligence grow as the individual matures? An intelligent child will grow up to be an intelligent adult, but what aspects of intelligence change as he grows? How is a mentally retarded adult like a child? How not like a child? How would a higher IQ help an adult adjust to a disability that comes in later life? How can a higher IQ create problems or stress for an individual? How can a higher IQ reduce problems or stress for an individual?

Lesson Plans

Photo pages

See Lesson Plans in Chapter 2 for guidelines to using the photo pages for this chapter.

IQ Testing (grades 4 -12)

Objective: To familiarize students with the standard systems for measuring intelligence, to help students understand how intelligence is related to all human functioning, not only academics.

Timeframe: 2 - 3 class periods.

Steps:

1. Talk to your school psychologist, educational diagnostician, or a psychologist in your community, to find out how to obtain sample questions for IQ tests. These professionals can probably supply you with some written information about IQ testing.

2. Invite a psychologist to speak to the class. Have your students compile questions to find out more about the test. Sample questions include: How was the system developed? How are the questions cho-

sen? How can the test be standard, i.e., how can it apply to everyone in a similar way? What are the fluctuations in scoring? Can an individual score differently on different days? Does age affect the score? Does stress affect the score?

3. Have the students write their own sample questions, using the principles of the standard tests as a guide. Administer the homemade test to the class.

4. Discuss the concept of intelligence, using the Ideas for Discussion section above. You might introduce the idea of the bell curve, which illustrates how the majority of people fall within a central range of intelligence, with smaller proportions of the population falling in the end ranges, genius and mentally retarded.

Sensitivity Training for Learning Disability (grades 4–12)

Objective: To develop sensitivity in students for people with
    learning disability, and appreciation for challenges they face.
Timeframe: Two class periods.
Steps:
1. Have the class separate into small groups of 3 - 6 students.
2. Have each group take a textbook and choose any chapter. The assignment is to rewrite one page by altering the letters of the words, with the intention of simulating the way words and sentences appear to someone with a reading disability. For example, change every "b" to a "d," replace every "e" with an "a," remove every "h," exchange every "of" for "if" or "in," exchange every "w" for "m," etc. It is very important to be consistent in the changes. Choose one or two alterations, and apply them throughout the page to every occurrence of those letters or words.
3. Have the groups exchange their rewritten pages. Class members can take turns reading aloud.
4. Discuss the exercise. Did any students feel frustrated or embarrassed when they tried to read? Did it make them angry, or did they feel like quitting? How would they have felt if someone was telling them to hurry up, or calling them stupid? Were any students able to figure out what the changes were, and apply it to other words as they went? Discuss how this sometimes happens with people with reading disability; they learn to pronounce the sound for "b" even though they

still see it as a "d." In effect, they learn new rules, not based on phonetics, but on memorized letters and sounds.

5. Other exercises include:

a. Wear two pairs of rubber gloves while trying to write, tie shoes, button a shirt, or accomplish some other fine motor skill activity.

b. Try playing catch with a ball, using your non-dominant hand and closing one eye.

c. Looking in a mirror, write your name on a piece of paper. Do not look at the paper, but only in the mirror.

d. Button a shirt with one hand.

e. Take a large spoonful of peanut butter onto the roof of your mouth and read aloud.

Terminology (grades 8–12)

Objective: to increase students' awareness of correct and incorrect usage of terms applying to disability.

Timeframe: One class period.

Steps:

1. Introduce the class to the categories listed in this chapter which are used for defining the disabilities of students in special education. Discuss each type of disability and how it might manifest in an individual. If you are aware of students in your school who have one or more of these disabilities, use them as an example. This will help students connect the terms with actual names, faces, and conditions.

2. Next, have the students come up with as many slang names as possible for someone with a disability. A term such as "retard" stems from mental retardation. Encourage the students to be honest and objective in creating the list. There is no need to be embarrassed, because these words really do exist in our society, and are used in very negative ways. Discuss how name-calling often results from fear and dislike, and how it reinforces the separation between two groups of people. For example, if students are calling each other "retard" as an insult, they will most likely be very uncomfortable around someone who actually has retarded mental development.

3. Once you have a list, match the slang terms with the definitions, to see which categories they fall into. Note which categories have the

most negative terms associated with them. Is it the physical or the mental disabilities? Ask the students if they think mental disability is more threatening or frightening to people than physical, or is it the other way around? Take a survey: would the students rather be blind or deaf? What are the benefits and drawbacks to the different limitations?

4. Have the students create a list of disability categories and a short definition of each. Under each listing, include the slang terms. The list can be copied onto a piece of poster board and posted in a school hallway, so that other students can also learn about the relationship between slang terms that are unconscious or insulting, and the correct terms for disabilities.

Guest Speaker (grades 4–12)

Objective: To introduce students to types and definitions of
disabilities that are seen in classmates and peers.
Timeframe: One class period.
Steps:
1. Invite a special education teacher to speak to your class.
2. Request the speaker to tell the class about several different students in the school who have visible, severe, or moderate disabilities. Have the speaker address the type of disability, and whether it manifests in varying forms and degrees. If the class has made a listing of disability definitions (Terminology lesson plan), ask the speaker to use it as a reference in talking about a specific individual's disability.
3. Have the speaker also tell about how the definitions are used in determining what kind of help and support a student will need to get the most out of school.
4. Encourage the students to ask questions.
5. Have the students write a thank-you note to the special education speaker.

Creative Writing (grades 6–12)

Objective: To develop creative writing skills; to encourage students
to consider another person's life experience; to have students
identify qualities of character necessary in certain situations.

Timeframe: One to two class periods. (This can be a homework assignment that is discussed in class after completion.)

Steps:

1. Give the students the following instructions for their writing assignment: Pretend you have a disability. Tell what the disability is and describe your abilities and limitations. Then tell a story about going into a public situation and what happens. If you meet someone, describe the interaction. How do they treat you? Do you make a friend or have a negative experience? How do you handle any difficult moments? How is the story resolved?

2. Discussion or follow-up assignment can include having the students discuss their characters. Did he or she have fear or shame? Did they act with courage? What was challenging for the character? What was helpful for them?

Research paper (grades 9–12)

Objective: To familiarize students with people with disability who have made significant contributions to society.

Timeframe: Approximately four weeks.

Steps:

1. Have students research famous people with disability. A good resource for this information is the Internet. They might also contact a local association or independent living center to obtain lists of people. See Appendix: Famous People with Disability, and Recommended Resources.

2. If a biography is not available, have them gather information from newspaper or magazine articles.

3. After writing a research paper of a length determined by the teacher, students can also present oral reports on their famous person in class. Encourage use of photographs that show the disability if it is visible.

Student Biography: Nando

5.1: Nando

Nando's disability is called Down's Syndrome. This disability causes mental retardation in people, also called intellectual impairment, which means the person's mental abilities do not fully develop. Even as he grows older, Nando will act and think like a child. Down's Syndrome can happen to any baby, but it's more common if the mother is older than 35 years old when she has the baby.

Figure 5.1 Nando (photo by Ted Schooley).

Down's Syndrome also affects the way a person looks, and many people with Down's have similar facial features: a broad forehead, a round flat face, shallow eye sockets, and a protruding lower jaw. You have probably seen other people who look like Nando; very likely they have Down's Syndrome. Certain personality traits seem to go along with this disability as well, for example many people with Down's are affectionate and loving much of the time. They can also be very stubborn.

Nando can be extremely stubborn when he doesn't want to do something. He puts his arms across his chest and won't talk. He acts like a little child, which can be very frustrating for the people caring for him. On the other hand, children can be fun to be with, and so is Nando. He loves to laugh, to tickle people, and to sing. He clowns around to be funny.

Nando doesn't seem to get depressed about having Down's Syndrome; he probably isn't fully aware that he is different from other people. If he is accepted and people are friendly to him, he's happy. He wants to be more independent, to have adults let him do more things on his own, but he's not capable enough to be given a lot of freedom. He could easily get into trouble.

Questions:

1. How do most people express anger appropriately when they get older?

2. What kinds of trouble might Nando get into if he's not supervised?

5.2: Jumping Rope

Here Nando is exercising, which is important to him for two reasons: it helps him learn coordination so he has better use of his body, and it helps keep him healthy because the Down's Syndrome makes him overweight. Students with disability come to school to learn more than just the academic subjects. Working on their bodies is part of their educational program.

If you told Nando he had to stop jumping rope before he was ready to, he might get very upset. He doesn't like to be interrupted when he's focused on something. If he were really mad, he might call you an animal name, which is his way of expressing anger. He acts so mad that it can be funny. He doesn't realize how silly he appears to others. His teachers have learned how to handle his anger and stubbornness by holding up two fingers and saying, "Nando, you have two choices: you can do your work now, or I'll call your parents and you can go home." Usually he does his work, and the anger is quickly forgotten. Occasionally the teacher has to call his parents to come get him; then he feels bad because he knows he's done the wrong thing. He really does want to please people.

Figure 5.2 Jumping Rope (photo by Bill Davis).

Questions:

1. Does it seem fair to you that Nando will graduate from high school without taking regular academic courses?

2. What other activities might be part of Nando's educational program?

3. Does your anger ever get the better of you, where you make the wrong choice just to be stubborn? How do you overcome your anger in order not to get into trouble?

5.3: Fine Motor Skills

Besides having less mental ability, Nando has trouble using his hands to do fine skills or small work. Writing is one way of learning hand coordination. His writing is very elementary: days of the week, numbers, his name. He can recognize certain words but cannot read a sentence. He enjoys writing and works well on his own when he likes the work.

Figure 5.3 Fine Motor Skills (photo by Bill Davis).

After a while, his work of writing letters turns into writing rows and rows of loopy squiggles, like a child pretending to write in script. Many people with Down's Syndrome do exactly the same thing. It might be a way of calming themselves with the repeated movement of the hand and pen, like rocking back and forth.

At home, Nando has certain chores and responsibilities. He cleans his bedroom, washes dishes, scrubs the sink. He loves eating and can make a simple lunch. It would be possible for Nando to be a cook's helper as a job when he graduates, or to wrap hamburgers and serve fries at a fast food restaurant. He would need to be closely supervised for about a month until he got used to the routine, but once he learns the job, he can do it fine.

Questions:

1. What is the difference between being able to recognize a word, and reading?

2. Do you think many restaurant managers would be willing to take the time to train and supervise Nando? Why would they bother, if they could get faster workers?

3. Why is it important for people to feel productive, even if they are very limited in their abilities?

5.4: Woodshop

Nando loves working on projects, such as sanding a piece of wood in shop. Since he needs a lot of supervision, Nando will probably never live on his own. However, he could live in a group home with other people who have disabilities. Often these group homes have businesses that earn money, like running a greenhouse. Nando could easily learn to plant seeds, pull weeds and water flowers. Adult workers supervise the people with disabilities to make sure they're taking care of themselves and getting their work done. The workers take the people shopping or to the movies. It's very much like having parents around, but Nando would get as much freedom and independence as he could handle. And, most important, he could be an active member of his community, just like most other people.

Figure 5.4 Woodshop (photo by Bill Davis).

Right now Nando is very happy to live at home with his parents and sister. He loves being part of the family, and participating in all the celebrations and traditions. On Sunday's, the family has a rule of no television. This is their way of making the Sabbath a special day, different from the other days of the week. One Sunday morning Nando found his father watching TV with no sound. He walked up and turned off the TV, telling his dad that he shouldn't break the rules. Like a child, he takes a rule very seriously, something you always obey. He doesn't understand the idea of "stretching" a rule.

Questions:

1. What does it mean to stretch a rule? What rules do you stretch sometimes? How do you decide which you can stretch and which you can't?

2. What will Nando like about living in a group home? What do you think he'll miss about being at home?

5.5: School Work

Can you see in the photo the stubborn look on Nando's face? His teacher is giving him a choice of which work he will do, and it takes him a long time to decide. He may not want to do any of it. Teachers have to be very patient with a student like Nando, giving him lots of time to understand and learn. It's a whole different way of teaching.

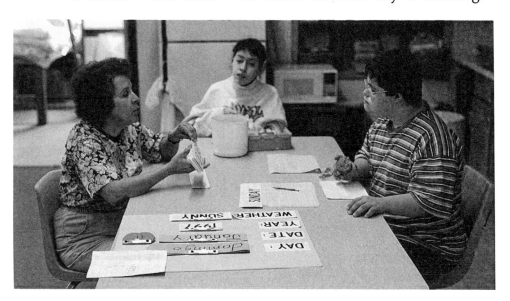

Figure 5.5 School Work (photo by Bill Davis).

Even when Nando wants to learn something, it takes him a long time. He has to do the same thing over and over, and eventually he knows how. In school he learns to read words that will help him when he graduates. For example, he learns to follow simple directions on food boxes such as macaroni and cheese. He learns to recognize the word "poison" on a label.

Last fall, Nando helped his class plant tulip bulbs. He knew that they had to be buried six inches deep, so he dug each hole and used a ruler to measure the depth. Much of what Nando learns is to help him take care of himself and to function as well as he can on his own.

Questions:

1. How is teaching Nando different than teaching you? What kinds of training do you think special education teachers need?

2. How would it be to take care of someone who looks like a teenager but acts like a child? How would you have to adjust your own behavior?

3. When you don't feel like doing schoolwork, how do you behave?

Chapter 6

PROJECT-BASED INCLUSION

In many schools, students with severe and profound disability spend most of their school days in a self-contained classroom. They are unable to participate in the regular academic program for their age, because they need more services than can be provided in a general ed setting, even with the help of an aide or a modified curriculum. These are the students most in need of being exposed to the normal, age-appropriate, everyday activities that are naturally taken for granted by general ed students. Going to a basketball game, playing catch during recess, watching a movie, sharing a pizza – are just a few of the ways that kids hang out together and have fun. Few opportunities exist for students with disability to be included in these simple activities, because they are kept with others who are more "like them." Authentic social interaction with a wide variety of peers is desperately needed to enable these students to develop self-esteem and a sense of belonging to a larger community beyond the world of disability.

What Is Project-Based Inclusion?

Project-based inclusion is an effective and innovative approach to changing attitudes around disability, where the actual process of integrating students with and without disability evolves over time. Inclusion itself is the objective, not a secondary possibility. With project-based inclusion, attitudes are examined consciously, rather than putting students together and hoping for the best. Inclusion becomes a project instead of a placement, a perspective instead of an educational plan. This method focuses on two full groups of students rather than one special ed student placed within a group of general ed students. Increased acceptance and awareness is accomplished by incorporating the groups as a team, coming together around a specific project with beginning and end dates, a sequence of events and activities, and a final goal. The classes are integrated for a period of time each day, or each week, during which they get to know each other and develop an expanded level of comfort being together. Specific steps are outlined to educate the general ed students about disability, in order to decrease fears, eliminate misconceptions, and promote understanding based on factual information. The setting created by project-based inclusion offers an authentic environment for friendship and communication. Activities are kept at a level that all can enjoy, thus preventing the danger of shame or inferiority for students whose skills are limited. The primary target population of project-based inclusion is the students participating in the project. Secondarily, this method is capable of educating on a community-wide basis: the larger school body, parents and other teachers, and even a portion of a town or city. Project-based inclusion, PBI, draws from several contemporary and tested teaching approaches which are crucial for shaping an inclusion project.

Service Learning is both a philosophy and a methodology. With service learning, the regular curriculum is augmented with out-of-classroom, hands-on experiences which are usually of service to the community. Students work with an agency, individual business person, or community service in order to learn about different career/vocational choices. They are not necessarily paid for their work, but the long-term benefits include personal growth, improved self-esteem, and increased social responsibility. Service learning is most effective when the students have an opportunity to examine and talk about their experiences on a regular basis with a mentor, teacher, or other involved adult. In PBI, artists, writers, and other professionals work with students, teaching crafts and skills that relate to the specific project. Inclusion projects can be designed to be of service to the community, such as programs for elders, young children, or educational productions for the general public.

Cooperative Education, also known as Peer Education, applies to grouping students of differing abilities, in order to increase academic performance and self-esteem. Students work together in small groups, with the stronger academic students providing guidance and information to others who are less advanced. Assignments are often shared by the group, requiring individual participation if the whole group is to succeed. The "work-together-as-a-group" nature of this arrangement allows slower students to observe and follow those with academic leadership abilities. The teamwork needed for PBI relies strongly on this model of cooperative interaction.

Peer Tutoring implies a one-to-one relationship, student to student, to offer assistance on a particular subject. As with Cooperative Education, students are brought together to dissolve possible separations based on academic standards. It provides an opportunity for sharing and helping, without the stigma of failure or incompetence. It also encourages friendships to form, as a result of the time spent together over several weeks or months. Students with disability often work very well with the Peer Tutoring approach, where their "teacher" is a peer. This model is also an integral part of a successful inclusion project, because students get to know each other on a real and personal level. Whether one-to-one or class-wide, these methods bring students together in an alternative setting requiring communication and interaction.

PBI: A Two-Way Street

One of the most unique aspects of project-based inclusion is the concept of two-way education. The benefits of integrating students with and without disability belong to both groups. General ed students have to learn new ways of communicating, often quite different from their accustomed use of words and hand gestures. They may need to listen more carefully to unusual speech patterns, use sign language or body language, and generally be more attentive to how someone with differences is getting the message across. They discover that they can indeed communicate with students they thought incapable of communication. Fear of difference dissolves as they begin to see past the stereotype of disability to the individual person inside. On the other hand, students with disability have a chance to discover and share in the activities, fun and social patterns of their peers, from which they were often left out. Through peer responses and feedback, students with disability can develop an enhanced social sense. A single negative comment from a peer about inappropriate behavior is often more effective than weeks of instruction by a teacher. In fact, each group can observe and learn from appropriate and inappropriate behaviors in others. Fun and productive time together measurably increases students' acceptance of each other and reduces the tension that commonly accompanies differences.

Teachers also benefit from project-based inclusion. In most schools, students with severe disability are frequently viewed by classroom teachers as the most undesirable and difficult students. Such attitudes may be partly due to lack of adequate training for teachers, and partly due to unconscious attitudes. This book has explained many of the reasons behind this situation, and now offers a remedy. Project-based inclusion gives general ed teachers the chance to get to know students who are different, without suddenly being responsible for them within the daily classroom. PBI is a "first step" for everyone, toward the eventual goal of successful inclusion throughout the school and throughout society. Viewing acceptance as a two-way process is the foundation of project-based inclusion. Everyone is a teacher, and everyone has something to learn.

A Least Restrictive Environment

A basic component of the Individuals with Disabilities Education Act states that students should receive their education in the "least restrictive environment." In other words, all students are to be educated with as little specialized help as possible, while still accessing a full and equal level of educational opportunity. Two concerns determine a student's least restrictive environment: (1) academic: that students with disability receive an education appropriate to their unique learning needs and abilities, and (2) social: that the education takes place in as close proximity as possible to nondisabled, similar age-level peers. Social interaction between students with and without disability is encouraged by this law, requiring teachers and other personnel to "assure, to the maximum extent possible, that disabled children are educated with children who are not disabled." The academic requirement can override the social objectives in some cases. When the nature or severity of the disability indicates that the student cannot be properly educated within a general ed class, then the issue of peer proximity takes a back seat.

Project-based inclusion addresses the social integration component of the least restrictive environment mandate. As a philosophy, PBI embraces three essential goals:

• to improve the social competence of students with disability;

• to improve attitudes of students who will become parents, taxpayers and service providers in a society which includes people with disability;

• to improve awareness of teachers who will increasingly be asked to incorporate students with disability into general ed classes.

Students and teachers who participate in an inclusion project do change their attitudes about disability, without having to suffer through fear, discomfort and uncertainty. Even students who are not cognitively capable of spending part of their school days in a general ed program can often participate in PBI. Comprehensive support is maintained during all PBI activities, unlike full inclusion where general and special ed teachers are often placed together with little preparation, training, planning time or sufficient support staff. PBI offers a truly inclusive and nonrestrictive environment.

Preliminary Steps

Project-based inclusion begins with a team, and depends heavily on good working relationships between the professionals involved. Shared goals, visions, and enthusiasm will make an inclusion project fun and ensure success. Chapter 7, Team Building, offers teachers some elementary pointers on forming and sustaining a strong team. The first two members of the team are ideally a general ed teacher and a special ed teacher of students who have severe disability and are usually not involved with general ed activities. The two classes are the beginning elements for the project.

The next step is defining a community or school need. Most communities have a fundamental need to increase understanding and acceptance of people who live with disability. The project itself integrates students with severe disability into the community in a visible and positive way. Identifying a community need is a task that the two teachers decide upon together, taking into account the type of community in which they live, the types of students in the classes, and the amount of funding and time available. A PBI project could be:

• Putting on a play about disability issues for the school or the public

• Planting and tending a community garden during fall and spring months on or near school grounds

• Starting a clothing bank for the school or larger community
• Opening a school store
• Weekend programs for the elderly, such as skits, music, or games
• Making a video about disability issues in the school or community

Once a project is chosen, it's time to gather a small team of interested people. The foregoing list of sample projects makes it clear that professionals from the community will be very helpful. A writer or theater person might help produce a play; a local nursery might donate plants or advice about gardening; a church or community group might be willing to provide a room for a clothing or food bank. Numerous resources exist in every community, and their participation will enrich the project in many ways.

Getting Started

Now it's time to begin the project. It is unreasonable to assume that students without disability will feel comfortable around students with disability (or vice versa), just by putting them in the same room together. This applies to project personnel as well. Thorough planning for the foundation of the project is essential to eventual success. The first couple of months will probably be geared toward introducing the two groups through different activities and lots of education. Here is a sample timeline for promoting comfortable interaction:

Week One: Students in general ed are informed about the upcoming project, including details about the project itself as well as the more fundamental goal of integrating the two classes. The students take the Self-Assessment Survey (Chapter 2) and have at least one class discussion about how they feel around people with disability. Discussion can include sharing of stories about friends, relatives, or any experience of disability familiar to the students.

Week Two: Students in general ed have a guest speaker from the community who has a disability (see Lesson Plans, Chapter 2). The speaker shares his or her experience of having a disability. Ask the speaker to give factual information about the disability, as well as subjective information on experiences and feelings. Follow-up to the speaker is a lesson plan from one of the chapters in this book, such as a sensitivity training session (spending a day in a wheelchair) or other assignment to promote awareness and thoughtfulness. Special ed students are being prepared by informing them of the upcoming project and its goals.

Week Three: The special ed teacher/team leader gives presentations to the general ed class about each of the students with disability with whom they will be working on the project. Information includes how the student became disabled, what his or her life is like today, what the capabilities and limitations are, and how to best communicate with him or her. Photographs help students begin to identify their peers with disability as individuals. Questions from the general ed students are encouraged. Continue preparing the special ed class with more simple and basic information on how the project will be accomplished.

Week Four: The two groups come together for an "ice-breaker" activity. A little party with snacks, meeting in the gym to play catch, and listening to music during a free time, are all ways to create a relaxed and open environment. Team teachers play a key role here, as they begin introducing students to each other and initiating conversation or communication. Don't worry if things feel uncomfortable–they probably will! Over time, the discomfort will fade; this is only the first step. It's also very important to have a de-briefing session with each class, asking the students how the activity felt, what they noticed, ways in which they were uncomfortable, or any other feelings they observed in themselves or others.

Week Five: Two or three guest speakers visit (on separate days) the combined classes, to present on an aspect of disability or special ed. Choices include: physical therapist, special ed department head, speech therapist, occupational therapist, medical doctor, or psychologist. Each speaker will be asked to give information about how they work with disability, and share what they know about creating positive attitudes. For example, a physical therapist might dispel notions that someone with cerebral palsy is in pain, or that receiving physical therapy is painful. A speech therapist can explain that many people who cannot speak nonetheless understand others perfectly well, and give ideas for increasing communication with someone who does not speak well, or at all. An occupational therapist might demonstrate how certain adaptive equipment is used, such as adapted forks or utensils. The presence of both groups of students will help to further the bonding process, as disability becomes something that is "okay" to talk about, not something hidden or shameful.

Week Six: Bring the two groups together for another activity, perhaps learning a folk dance with the help of a community member, or making clay objects. Students without disability will be asked to help their peers who are not able to work alone. Have another speaker during this week also. Team teachers stay very involved, ensuring that students with disability get the help they need, and helping general ed students learn to approach and interact with their peers.

Week Seven: General ed students are separated into groups of three or four. Size of the groups will depend on how many students are in the classes; each special ed student will be assigned to a general ed group. Students in the general ed groups design activities to do with their special ed student. They must take into consideration the limited abilities of the student with whom they will be working. Examples of shared projects could be: helping a student shoot a basketball; reading a story to a student; playing a simple game like bingo or matching cards; putting on make-up or nail polish; fixing a hairdo; coloring; playing hopscotch. The students can design their activities early in the week, and report to the class about their plans. Later in the week the groups come together to put the projects into practice. By this time, teachers may begin to notice more eye-contact between students, maybe some laughter or joking, and in general the beginnings of a relaxed environment.

Week Eight: Perhaps bring in another guest speaker, such as the parent of a student with disability, another professional, or another community member with disability. Continue using lesson plans involving movies, creative writing, or speakers, to further educate the classes. The chapter content and lesson plans throughout this book are specifically structured for this exact purpose, to awaken people out of old perspectives.

This timeline gives a good picture of the careful planning that supports the development of true relationship between the two classes. Without this step-by-step introduction, there is a risk of students losing interest. Facing one's discomfort is not an easy challenge. Teacher support is imperative to allow students a range of reactions. At all times students must know they will find respect, acknowledgment, and acceptance for expression of their fears and hesitations. Some students will obviously be more willing and open than others in this process. Allow students to learn and grow in their own time; be encouraging but never forceful or critical. Often the simplicity and open friendliness of students with disability can win over even the "coolest" of general ed students.

The Project

During this introductory period, plans for the project can begin to unfold. As teachers talk to their classes about the project, they will begin identifying which students are interested in which aspects. Students in both classes need to feel like a part of the project. Get excited! Enthusiasm on the part of the team leaders is contagious. Encourage the sharing of ideas to enhance the project; this will help students take ownership of the outcome. Assign responsibilities to those students who will commit and get the job done. Teachers can decide whether participation in the project will be graded. Structuring the project as schoolwork for credit can help stimulate students' response and commitment.

Not all teachers will have access to an individual with disability who is willing to be on the project team. If possible, this added element can be enormously helpful. A person with disability who is verbal and able to be present throughout the project provides a kind of bridge to connect the various groups: students with disability, students without disability, teachers, professionals, and the public. This individual can greatly enhance the project by speaking about personal experiences with disability, by promoting public awareness of the project, and by offering insight and guidance to ensure that the project remains sensitive and focused on the issues of disability. An individual who is able to communicate well functions as a visible role model for students with and without disability.

Involving other community support people will help spread the word about the project. The more people throughout the community that hear about this project, the better! Look for opportunities to take the students out together, for a soda or a walk in the park. Seek funding from banks, car dealerships, restaurants, and other businesses, partly to raise money, and partly to create community awareness. Ask the local newspaper to do a feature article as the project begins to develop. Parents may wish to get involved also. A letter sent home with students can ask for specific types of talent and support: carpenters, photographers, cooks, seamstresses, artists, graphic designers, etc. Skills and talents abound in every community. As needs are identified for the project, don't be afraid to ask for help. Many people are pleased to be asked, and excited to see something innovative being done around the subject of disability.

Look for authentic ways to incorporate students with disability into the work. One option is to have students without disability help those with impairments to participate. Assisted participation means one student holds and guides the hand of another, to draw, paint, write, or otherwise take part in a creative activity. Someone in an electric wheelchair can carry signs or baskets. Someone who cannot walk well or speak might sit at a booth or table handing out materials. Many students, even those with severe limitations, are able to do some of the simple tasks that create the project. Of course, timeframes will need to be adjusted to allow for the slower pacing of most special ed students.

Inclusion projects easily take four to six months to accomplish. Beginning in late fall establishes a foundation before the holidays. This is a good time to work with bringing the groups together and getting them comfortable with each other. The central work of the project will be tackled during the late winter and spring semesters, culminating before the end-of-school pressures descend. Planning a timeline for the project will help prevent last minute anxieties.

The Outcome

Assessing the outcome of the project is one of the final components of organizing an inclusion project. Outcomes are important for several reasons:

1. To form a foundation for future projects.

2. To establish credibility with school administrators and funding sources.

3. To demonstrate the potential for dissolving barriers and changing attitudes.

4. To make the team feel good about their efforts.

However, sometimes measurable outcomes are harder to document than those witnessed informally by the participants. Teachers working with the students may observe many small, seemingly insignificant interactions that actually demonstrate the success of the project more clearly than numbers or statistics ever could. True success is seen in the day-to-day behaviors of those involved in the project. When a big, strong, football-playing student tells another football player to quit making fun of a student with disability, you know beyond doubt that the first student has truly learned something. When two general ed girls are talking and giggling with a girl from the special ed program, you know attitudes have been changed. These outcomes are perhaps the most significant, and should be included in any formal documentation, to truly record the nature of changes that were accomplished.

Written assessments do not need to be technical or detailed. An assessment is basically a summary of the project goals and how they were met. Examples of observations as those used above can be incorporated into the report. The report can be prepared by any of the team members, and compiled throughout, and at the end of, the project. It's a good idea to have someone keeping notes during the course of the activities, to record any incidents that illustrate new and open attitudes about disability. For example, during one project Manny, a boy from the special ed class, seemed to be missing during a lunch break. Team leaders were looking for him when one of the general ed students reported, "He went out to lunch with Josh and Michael." Josh and Michael happened to be two of the high school's best basketball players. Later Manny shared that this was the first time he had ever gone to lunch with "friends." Here was an event worthy of documenting.

The assessment might also include any goals that were not met, and explain what the obstacles were or why the course of the project was altered. Not meeting goals is not necessarily an indication of failure. It may mean that the original goals were found to be unrealistic, and adjusted to a more attainable standard. The report can note what was learned from not meeting certain objectives, and address changes that will make future projects more successful.

A final report on the project will also want to mention any ways the project will continue to impact the community. Can the project be a model for other schools or future years? Did a newspaper article or radio show inform a larger number of people about the project? Were any materials developed within the project that will be distributed to a greater audience or the public? These considerations significantly increase the impact of a project within a community.

One method commonly used to determine outcomes is the pretest and posttest. A test is administered to students prior to the project's inception, and then again after its completion. Results indicate whether attitudes changed and in which areas. We suggest the Self-Assessment Survey (Chapter 2) for a pretest. It could also be used again after the students have finished the project, and responses compared. A more specific posttest is included at the end of this chapter.

It can be altered or added to according to the particular group of students.

Start Small, But Start

Projects do not have to be large and involved to be effective. A one-semester project between classes, creating a display for the school hallway or community center, will take much less time, energy and money than a four month production. Yet it can still have a significant impact, especially on the students participating. Involving students with various levels of ability allows some to be more active in the process, and others to be included through their presence and observation. Even for the students unable to actually join in the activities, there is a sense of sharing and being a part of the group. A student who is only familiar with a self-contained class may be thrilled to be helped along the hall by a peer from the general ed class rather than a teacher. Just sitting at a desk in the general ed class, and hearing how the students talk to each other and to their teacher, will be a new experience for some of the kids with disability. All of these seemingly minor details are actually full of life-changing potential. Never underestimate the effect that a genuine experience will have on any of the students involved. The key word is "genuine;" the outcome is of real value when it is connected to the community. Students forget their differences because the task at hand provides a unifying element; rather than looking at each other, they are looking at the project goals. Next thing they know, someone they used to think of as weird is now fun and funny. And it happened without anyone telling them they "should" change.

General ed classes need to begin on a small scale, perhaps just a few weeks of studying disability, before tackling a joint project with a longer timeframe. The point is to start somewhere, and get the ball rolling in your school and district, for increased awareness and opportunities for inclusion.

Posttest

1. How did you feel when the teacher told you about the proposed project and who you'd be working with?

_____ I was excited.

_____ I didn't think it had anything to do with school or learning.

_____ I didn't like the idea at all.

_____ I thought it was a good idea because I always wanted to meet those students.

_____ I was nervous because I didn't know how to act with kids who have disability.

2. How did you feel when you first met the special ed kids?

_____ I didn't know what to say to them.

_____ I felt comfortable right away.

_____ I was afraid I could catch something from them.

_____ I found it hard to look at some of them.

_____ I could see that they had their own ways of communicating.

3. What was the hardest part about getting to know other kids who are so different?

_____ I couldn't just speak to them like I do to other students.

_____ My own discomfort was hard to handle.

_____ I was never sure if they could understand me.

_____ I don't always understand what they are trying to tell me.

_____ I was afraid I might say something wrong or hurt them if I tried to help.

4. What surprised you as you got to know the students with disability?

_____ I was surprised that I wasn't as afraid anymore.

_____ I was surprised that some of these kids actually have a sense of humor.

_____ I was surprised that someone who can't talk or walk can use eye contact to get a message across.

_____ I was surprised that someone who is so totally disabled can still be happy.

_____ I was surprised that they could do things and help make the project happen.

5. What would you tell other people who are afraid of people with disability?

_____ Nothing, because I think they should be afraid.

_____ That people with disability aren't really very different.

_____ That you can get over your fear.

_____ That it feels more comfortable once you get to know someone with a disability.

_____ That I am afraid, too.

_____ That there really isn't anything to be afraid of.

6. How do you feel now about the special ed kids?

_____ More comfortable and relaxed around the kids with disability.

_____ Not much different than before the project.

_____ I feel better with the kids I know, but still feel uncomfortable around other people with disability that I don't know.

_____ I like them but I feel very sorry for them.

_____ I still feel embarrassed because I can do so much and they can't.

7. Have you noticed changes in your own personal thoughts and attitudes?

_____ My thoughts and attitudes are much more open to people who look and act different.

_____ I still have a lot of uncomfortable feelings and thoughts when I see someone who has a disability.

_____ It's easier for me to look at someone who is disabled now, or go up and say hello, even if it's a stranger.

_____ I still think if I were disabled that I wouldn't want to live, life would be pretty bad.

_____ Now I think that if I became disabled I could handle it okay, even if it was hard at first.

8. How do you think this type of project affects the special ed kids?

_____ It helps them because they get to do fun things.

_____ It is bad for them, because it makes them feel inferior to kids in general ed.

_____ It gives them a chance to feel like a regular student.

_____ Maybe it's hard for them because they will always want to be involved in this kind of project, and they can't be.

_____ It helps them trust people without disability.
_____ It makes them more distrustful of people without disability.

9. Would you recommend this type of project to other classes?
_____ Yes   _____ No

10. Did this project help you become more aware and accepting of people with disability?
_____ Very much
_____ A little bit
_____ Not at all
_____ It actually made me feel more uncomfortable.

11. What kind of long-term effects could this project have on you or others who were involved?

_____

_____

_____

_____

_____

12. Describe your feelings now when you see a person with disability in public.

_____

_____

_____

_____

_____

Students Together

6.1: Eating Together

The students in this special ed classroom can either eat in the cafeteria or have their lunches brought to the room. Often they prefer to eat in the classroom because they're uncomfortable eating in front of others. Their feelings are not unsociable; it's because they're self-conscious about things like chewing with their mouths open, or dropping food, or wearing a bib. All these problems are due to the disabilities, which make life a little more difficult for kids like Raymond, Felicia and Nathan. Of course they'd love to be sitting around a cafeteria table with all the other students.

Figure 6.1 Eating Together (photo by Bill Davis).

Nathan and Felicia can feed themselves. Nathan uses a spoon with a built up handle, which is easier for him to grasp. His food must be soft, like pudding or mashed potatoes, or else be cut up into very small pieces because he doesn't have good use of the mouth and jaw muscles needed for chewing. Felicia can chew but mostly her mouth is open and you can see all of the food in it. We all know this is not a polite way to eat, but it's the only way Felicia can chew, so she has no choice. She's aware that it's unattractive to others, and so she would rather stay in the privacy of the classroom with friends who truly understand and accept her disability. Raymond is a very fussy eater. Eating is not his favorite thing to do, and it's hard to get him to finish a meal. Raymond uses a special spoon that is held on his palm with an elastic strap. Sometimes people feed him if he's tired.

Suggestions: Invite a special ed class or several students to share a meal with your class, cooking together or ordering pizzas. Discuss how you and your classmates will make the special ed kids feel comfortable and welcome. Discuss how you might feel or act if some of those kids chew with their mouths open, or drool. Many people with disability seem mentally impaired, but are still very sensitive if someone is pointing at them or whispering about them.

6.2 Helping Others

Nando loves to push wheelchairs. He also likes to get in them and be wheeled around, whenever he can find an empty one. Raymond has a hard time pushing his own wheelchair, so it's a perfect combination when these two friends come together. Nando needs adult supervision when he's pushing, because he isn't always aware of safety issues, like a small step that could tip the chair.

Many young people with disability are especially helpful and giving to others. Maybe they realize how much help they get from others, and want to give back in return. Maybe they understand from their own experience that we all need help in one way or another, so they are eager to give what they can.

You might think that people who can't use their bodies fully would feel bothered if they had to help someone else. Even when it takes extra effort, most of these students you're learning about are very willing to help a classmate eat, or carry something, read a story to a friend who can't read, or help put a coat on.

We usually think of people with disability as being needy—they're the ones that need help. It may surprise you to learn that there's another side to disability: a very generous attitude that doesn't criticize others for needing help.

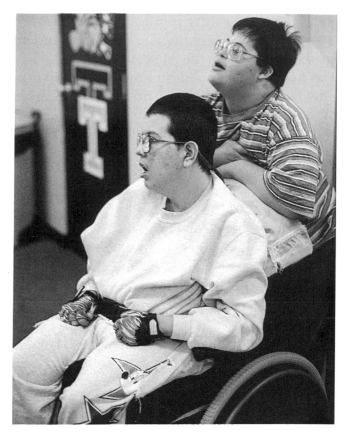

Photo 6.2 Helping Others (photo by Bill Davis).

Suggestions: Check with the special ed teacher, to find out if any of the students need help getting to a class, lunch, or somewhere else. Your class could volunteer to take turns helping a student. Or you could set up a time to read to the special ed students each week. Maybe two of you could do it together, if that would make you feel more comfortable at first.

6.3: Friendship

Neither Nathan or Felicia can speak. It's curious to think of a friendship without conversations. Much of it is based on their shared experiences, being together in school since they were very young. They've been together almost every day for so long that they are very close, like family. They can read the moods and feelings of each other, and share a sense of humor through eye contact and laughter. Sometimes they hug or shake hands; sometimes they make sounds and hand motions to each other. It's a very different way of relating and communicating; it might be hard for you to even imagine.

Friendship is very important to people with disability, maybe more so than for people who have full use of their bodies and minds. People with disability are so often stared at or rejected. They can feel isolated or lonely. Having friends is a part of life most of us take for granted. But if other people were uncomfortable around you, and didn't know how to talk to you or understand you, how would you make new friends?

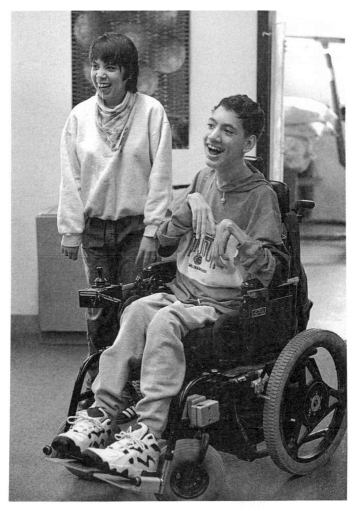

Figure 6.3 Friendship (photo by Bill Davis).

You might think ,"He probably doesn't have any friends because he can't do anything fun" or, "She can't speak so she can't have friendships." How wrong these statements are! As you've seen in these photos, people with disability do many fun things, know how to communicate, and enjoy having friends. Felicia and Nathan know that they are deeply accepted by each other, and that they share a friendship that they can trust. It gives them confidence in themselves when the time comes to reach out to make new friends.

Suggestions: Friendships begin when people are friendly to each other. Plan an activity that shows friendliness to the students with disability. It can be anything simple, even going to visit them in their classroom, or inviting them to yours for an informal get-together. Ask their teacher for suggestions on communicating with the kids. Do something that will help "break the ice" and make it easier to say hello in the school halls.

6.4: Dancing

Most teenagers love music, listening to the radio, going to concerts, and dancing.   But what do you do if your body doesn't move easily? When these students in the photo dance, it may not look like the way other people dance, it may be jerky or not exactly in time to the music. But dancing is really about feeling the music inside and letting your body respond. People with disability have the same feelings and enjoy the same pleasures. Some people in wheelchairs use the wheelchair to dance, tipping it back in wheelies and making it spin and dip. Others, who can stand but don't have a lot of movement, may rock back and forth. You could even dance with just your fingers, or swaying your head.

The students in this special ed class often go to the high school prom. Mostly they go together as a group, since it would probably feel uncomfortable to go alone. They very well might get teased or laughed at for their unusual body movements. They usually just dance in the classroom, where they feel safe. Some of the girls, like Felicia, would be thrilled to be asked to the prom by a boy, but there aren't many boys around who have learned to be comfortable around disability. Someday that will change, as people learn to look past the disability and see the beauty of the person inside: the joy, the humor, and the friendship.

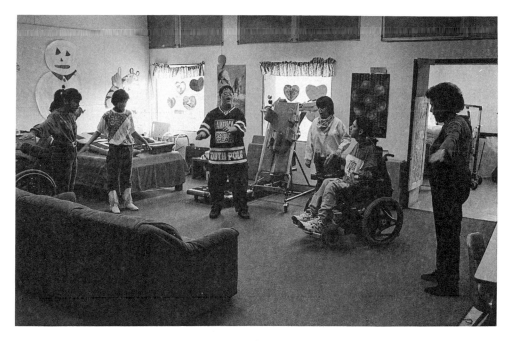

Figure 6.4 Dancing (photo by Bill Davis).

Suggestions: Asking kids with disability to dance in front of your class may be asking a lot. But if you had a little party with music and invited the special ed students, some of them might feel comfortable enough to join in. Another great way to share dancing is to find someone to teach both classes folk dancing, which is often very simple walking and stepping motions, clapping hands, turning, etc. You could help those who need guidance.

6.5: Creativity

Making things—creating—is one of the most rewarding activities we have as human beings. Whether we create a little birthday card for someone, paint a large beautiful picture, build a doghouse, or bake a batch of cookies, we are creating something new, something that expresses our ability. The ability doesn't have to be great or famous. It just feels good to look at what we've created and say "I made that."

Creativity is rewarding for students with disability and is often a part of their school work because it strengthens hand muscles and builds self-esteem. These girls at the table are each working on a project according to their abilities. One is using the sewing machine, which takes hand and eye coordination, as well as the mental ability to understand how the machine works and how to put the fabrics together. Another girl is doing a very simple task of threading yarn through holes in a paper plate to make a decoration. A third girl is putting together a little book with a cloth cover as a gift to some preschool children. Not all the girls can use the sewing machine, and some would be bored if their projects were too easy. Each one needs just the right challenge for their abilities. Many people famous for their creations and discoveries had some sort of disability that we don't even know about. Disability does not have to get in the way of creativity, and people with disability enjoy the pleasure of seeing their finished work, just like you do.

Figure 6.5 Creativity (photo by Bill Davis).

Suggestions: Plan a project time to share with the special ed students. Decide on an activity such as drawing, coloring, sewing, working with clay, pasting collages, etc. Some of the students will need help, very much like helping young children. Help those that need it, but also do your own project so you're all working together.

Chapter 7

TEAM BUILDING

The foundation of project-based inclusion is the team of players that make it happen. No single person is likely to have the strength, time or desire to organize a comprehensive project geared toward educating the school or community. Therefore, creating a team is the first step. The importance of developing a team cannot be overemphasized, and for this reason an entire chapter is being devoted to the subject. Specific skills can enhance a teacher's ability to identify effective co-workers and to function supportively on a team, as well as help to avoid some of the more common pitfalls.

Team building can be one of the most challenging aspects of project-based inclusion. It can also be an enjoyable and educational experience. However, without shared effort and common vision, people soon end up going in different directions. Unfortunately, those directions usually reflect personal agendas and self-serving interests that divert energy from the original intention of educating the school population or larger community on the issue of disability.

History has demonstrated that higher goals, regardless of the specific issues they center around, are perhaps the only thing capable of uniting diverse groups. And since disability crosses all boundaries—gender, age, economic, social, religious, and ethnic—this effort ideally will incorporate a wide variety of people. A project-based inclusion team must represent a number of groups: parents, students, teachers, community professionals, community members with disability, and school administration personnel. Finding the right people, developing a workable plan, and executing it with the least amount of conflict and confusion, will take considerable dedication and determination, usually stemming from one or two key players who will manage to keep the whole team functioning well, or at least well enough. The interplay of personalities, talents, energies, and ages inevitably creates a rich experience full of fun, learning, frustration, and camaraderie. The ultimate success of the project might be reflected more in the ability of the team to work together, than in the achievement of particular results.

What Makes a Team?

Webster's dictionary defines the word team as "a group of people working or playing together, especially as one side in a contest." Additional definitions refer to being yoked or harnessed together, as with two or more horses or oxen, and also to cooperative activity. The term teamwork is defined as "joint activity by a group of people, in which each person subordinates his individual interests and opinions to the unity and efficiency of the group." These definitions reveal the essential nature of a team: the members must be coordinated, joined, and jointly addressing the same task. It does not necessarily have to be a contest, but there is usually the inherent concept of accomplishing a goal.

Let's look at some of the ingredients that ensure an effective team.

Unity

Unity is the building block of a team, the element that enables individuals to identify with the larger group and its mission. Language becomes "we" instead of "I." Jobs get delegated and shared, rather than falling on one or two people. Attention is focused on the project, not on the names or faces of key players.

The image of being yoked together clearly brings up the idea of unity. A yoke doesn't care whether the Old Gray Mare and Mr. Ed get along while plowing the corn field. They are in it together to get the job done. The yoke says, "You're going ahead, together, and you can either argue or laugh, it doesn't matter to me." The yoke provides the context of the work and the direction; it is a framework that arises out of the task at hand. On the other hand, a yoke can certainly feel like a lack of freedom, and stir up the reactionary impulse for individual authority. Subordinating one's personal will and interest to the larger goals of the group does not always feel admirable; sometimes it can be a very painful effort. Knowing when to subordinate, and when to try to guide the group in a new direction, can be a tricky question. And sometimes going against the flow can be the most productive act in bringing the group to a new level of unity.

Unity holds a higher priority than project success, because a project that is completed at the expense of relationships, friendships, and peace of mind is hardly a successful project. In the best of cases, when people get along with each other, have open communication, and share responsibility fairly, unity evolves and is quite enjoyable. But in other situations, unity can be sorely lacking, and needs to be cultivated and encouraged. The topic of unity should never be shied away from. The more it is spoken about and agreed upon, the more likely it will be number one on the "to do" list. Without such a priority, teams can easily fall into the trap of backbiting, resentment, and gossip. Getting the project done with this sort of underlying tension can hardly be called a success. Better to let the project remain incomplete, and maintain the ability to enjoy each other and the process.

Balance

In team building, balance refers to the balance of power and responsibility. The image of a mobile illustrates how each part must hang together to keep the whole mobile from being unevenly weighted. Even though some pieces may weigh more, or be larger than others, the relationship of the pieces—location and grouping—is what creates the effortless effect of floating and balance in a mobile. This is also true for a team; how the individual strengths and needs are utilized determines the effectiveness of the group. A strong team will be made up of individuals bringing together a number of talents, including leadership, work motivation, skills or professions relating to the project, organizational skills, conflict resolution techniques, humor, financial or record-keeping oversight, and creative abilities. Having a variety of skills on a team provides a healthy balance by distributing the work load and preventing burnout.

Another facet of balance is the give-and-take so necessary for working with team members. Each individual must find an inner balance between assertiveness and compliance. There are times when one must speak up, maybe even confront another team member about a sensitive subject. At other times, one must submit to a team decision, or a leadership decision, even when not in full agreement.

Leadership

Part of creating a successful balance of power is having proper leadership. This does not mean dictatorship, or the permission to be abusive or controlling. The leader of an inclusion team carries the responsibility of making final decisions in the event of an impasse, overseeing each team member's performance, and taking steps toward conflict resolution when needed. The paradox of good leadership is that it arises out of an ability to serve. An effective leader listens carefully to team members. Decisions are based on a knowledge of the team's needs and strengths, as well as the requirements of the project in terms of time, talent, personalities, and resources. Only by knowing his or her team members as individuals, not judging them or wanting them to be other than they are, can a leader perceive the best way to proceed, and which jobs to assign to whom. The role of leader is not an easy one. The glory of the position rarely equals the grief and frustration that almost inevitably come with the package. Ideally, the person leading the team will have good communication skills, a sense of interrelationships, and calm nerves.

Common Purpose

A common purpose or vision is another integral aspect of a team. Taking the time to actually formulate and write down the purpose of the project will aid significantly in uniting the team. It will also reveal at an early stage any differences of opinion regarding the purpose. The stated purpose should be brief and to the point, but well focused on the main concerns of the project. Wording of a statement of purpose is important. For example, the purpose might be: *To perform a skit about a famous person with disability, in order to provide an opportunity for meaningful relationships to develop between students in special ed and students in general ed classes.* This purpose indicates that the main focus is to perform a skit. If the team decides that the statement should center mainly around the development of relationships between students, it might be worded like this: *To develop meaningful relationships between students in special ed and students in general ed, by performing a skit, or organizing other activities.* When the purpose is clearly outlined as developing relationships, then excess anxiety and stress about the performance can be avoided. The team can stay focused on, "Are the students getting to know each other? Are relationships developing?" Purpose or mission statements can also number several objectives in order of importance. With project-based inclusion, the purpose should always relate first and foremost to the issue of inclusion in the real sense of bringing people together to know each other better. Keep the goal in mind as well as in speech and vision: talk about it, make slogans about it, think about it, and play with it.

Process-based

A process-based team differs from an outcome-based team, because it is willing to allow for changes that are integral to processes. Reaching the goal is a multilayered process, an unfolding string of events that is not always under control. It may seem paradoxical to say that a team must keep sight of the goal but not be attached to the outcome. Picture the goal as the mountaintop, and the process as the path that leads upward. There can be detours and deviations that still end up at the summit. How often a project, well-defined by the group at an early stage, turns out quite differently in the end. Processes have a way of taking their own course! Outcome-based projects focus solely on reaching a narrow and specific goal. Obstacles must be eliminated rather than learned from; the road that leads to the goal is not appreciated for itself. Much valuable experience can be lost with an outcome-based approach. To appreciate the process, it helps to relax into the unexpected or undesired circumstances that are guaranteed to arise. A healthy attitude is one that holds the vision of the goal, but allows the process to take detours in getting there. Keeping on track, without being too controlling of where the track goes, can be challenging, but well worth the effort. An element of trust is needed to recognize that the unfolding process is where most learning takes place. The actual outcome is more a by-product than the real meat of the project. Experience proves that everything usually ends up just right, with the goals being met more or less, even by a roundabout route.

Learning from the Pros

Sports teams, so familiar to most people in our country, provide an excellent illustration of a group of people working together toward a common goal. Games show how a team of players organize their abilities and actions to score more points than the opposing team. Their game is the "project" they've created. All the backstage tangles and tussles that went into the smooth operation of the game go unseen by the audience: the personality frustrations, the individual ambitions, the player who lacks motivation, the player who is dissatisfied with his position, the overbearing coach. The game is their profession, and they cannot get fed up and throw their project out the window. They have to get through the rough spots and find a way to present a unified effort. When a group of teachers comes together to work on a project, the same elements can surface. Team building is never as simple as coming up with a wonderful idea. Let's look at some of the rules that hold professional teams together and enable them to *Win!*

Show up for practice. If you don't show up, nothing can take place. You can't learn anything, change anything, accomplish anything. You can't even get rid of anything if you're not there! The show may go on without you, in which case you have no right to judge or recommend, or the show may not go on at all, because each person is a crucial player, without whom the structure fails.

Pass the ball. Even elementary school children learn this basic rule of team playing. No matter how talented, a team player has to think in terms of the team, by seeing the bigger picture. The person who appears least likely to succeed may just need a chance to learn. If no one passes the ball to that person, the chance will never come. When everyone is included as much and as often as possible, this also increases the likelihood of players showing up for practice. They won't get bored sitting on the bench.

Don't argue with the ump. Someone on the team must have the final say, even when it's a very difficult call. Discussions are essential, exploring every possible point of view, but when consensus cannot be reached the umpire gets to make the judgment, and the players live with the decision. This is a significant responsibility, so choose a leader carefully. And a bit of grumbling is natural just don't forget to show up for practice.

Big name players can have big ego needs. Star players may score high and please the audience with charismatic personalities, but they may be a pain in the neck to live with in the locker room or around the negotiating table. A player who is used to getting top billing may not want to share the glory, or may always claim to know the best way, better than everyone else. Exceptional skills may be accompanied by excessive self-centeredness. The skills may be valuable and necessary to the team, and usually the difficulties can be tolerated, with an occasional roll of the eyes and some good humor.

Choosing Your Team

Most projects begin with a single person. That person gets an idea and starts talking to other people about it. The other people may include friends, associates, other teachers, and related community members. As interest develops, a team begins to loosely form. It becomes evident who wants to participate and who will be a sideline supporter. Very often the formation of a team is informal; no firm commitments are made, no specific jobs are assigned, no mission statement is hammered out. It's just assumed, rather naively, that the group will work well together with compatible goals. Teams can easily evolve out of the initial period of excitement, for better or worse. Success is by chance, the result of luck or skills. On the other hand, the problems that plague many groups could be prevented with a bit of foresight in planning and carefully choosing team members and their positions. For the team leader, the one who wants to organize a team of people for a project, careful preparation time can avoid hours of future headaches.

Friendship is a good basis for working with someone. It doesn't have to be a friendship outside of school, but just to know that you enjoy someone's company is a good place to start. Have you had conversations with this person, beyond the small talk of a lunchroom table? Does he or she seem to share your views on disability? Does this person seem open to learning? Have you experienced any situations where you witnessed his or her approach to team participation? Would you call this person a team player, or is he or she more used to working alone? Is this someone you enjoy being around? This is a person you will be working closely with, perhaps under stress, and a personal connection can carry team members through rough times. The more you know about the person being considered for the team, the more accurately you will be able to judge the appropriateness of the choice.

Team members should also be sought for skills specific to the project. Being a good "team player" or being a friend is not quite enough to qualify someone for the particular job you're looking to fill. The person should bring along an ability to contribute to the project: organization, writing, design, interpersonal, financial, educational, and creative skills will all be needed. Make sure you're not looking to one or two people to supply all of the talent. If the choice is limited in terms of people with a particular skill, the team may have to bear with a difficult personality here or there. If the rest of the team is strong and cohesive, it will hold together despite an occasional ego display or negative undercurrent.

Team members with any kind of training or background in group work, conflict resolution, or mediation can bring enormous benefit to the team. In the first place, they will probably have an understanding of how to communicate well with others. In the second place, if problems do arise, they will be able to help the team effectively move toward a solution. This person can function as an in-house mediator, even with small issues. Dealing with issues in the early stages keeps them from growing into large obstacles.

Once you've identified several people who seem like they might be interested, dedicated, and willing, begin talking. Talk about everything you can think of that relates to the project and what might come up as a result. Develop a list of questions, major and minor, to really assess the way this team will work together, and what possible danger areas might occur. You might want to take the Self-Assessment Survey together (Chapter 2). Take time to explore individual positions. Talk as a group, and talk separately.

Some sample questions include: Do these people realistically have time in their schedules to participate and give quality attention to their roles? What are their views on disability? What are their strengths? What do they not like doing? How should meetings be structured? How often? What are their backgrounds in teamwork? Have they done similar projects? What did they learn? Was it successful, and did they enjoy it? One member might have scheduling conflicts for a few weeks; someone else might have to share the load during that time. Is this agreeable to the team? Another member might have small children and be unable to work in the evenings. Do other people agree to afternoon meetings?

Assessing team members will never fully eliminate future problems. The most important thing about talking and meeting together is that it sets a tone of responsibility and accountability for the members. If each member knows that the team is going to be run with attention and integrity, this will encourage commitment to attend meetings, to voice concerns, and to support team goals. The very first steps of forming a team lays the groundwork for what evolves later.

Using What's Been Learned

The team you build to guide the project can be seen as a prototype for the team you are aiming to build between students. One is like a microcosm of the other, and paying attention to the attitudes and behaviors that are forming the team will ultimately help form a new inclusive community within the school. Project-based inclusion is capable of breaking down barriers that have existed because of unconscious, separating attitudes. Such attitudes have been discussed throughout this book as they relate to people with disability. However, taking a closer look, the same attitudes exist between all types of people, for some of the same reasons. This section recalls some of the concepts that have been presented in earlier chapters, and points out how they can aid teachers in working together and accepting each other's differences.

Avoid stereotypes.

It seems so handy to throw someone into a limiting category, rather than making the effort to see the complexity of the life behind the behavior. For example, a visible disability often masks a person's true and full abilities to the casual observer. Only by getting to know someone with disability can one really appreciate the wholeness of the person. Disability gives a concrete reason to take the extra step of putting judgment aside and looking more carefully at a person's life. When yoked together with another team member, the same principles apply, with or without disability. "He's just so selfish." "She has never been very friendly." "He's such a people-pleaser." "She's too emotional." Chances are good that every team member is sincerely wanting to participate, even if they appear unproductive or uncooperative. There is probably a cause of the behavior that needs to be addressed and recognized, in order to allow communication to flow more smoothly. Stereotypes for people with disability are tremendously damaging to self-esteem and individual potential. This also holds true for people with any type of difference. The way they communicate, the way they go about getting their job done, their emotional responses and personal need for acceptance or approval, the demands of their home life and pressing schedules: all of these factors contribute to the manner in which people work on a team. Bridges can be built, and understanding can develop, when the bottom-line is acceptance and appreciation of diversity.

Be open and friendly.

Maybe someone's actions have confused you. You don't understand the intention behind the behavior or words. Recall the Exercise in Imagination (Chapter 2) when you met a young man in the supermarket whose speech was unintelligible. The success of the meeting lay in your open and friendly attitude, rather than fear and avoidance. Approaching a team member with an open and sincere attitude of wanting to communicate and listen (not just wanting to be agreed with) can profoundly change a working relationship. So much is lost between people due to misunderstandings that are never addressed. Expect the most out of others.

Develop awareness of unconscious attitudes.

As with attitudes about disability, there are unconscious attitudes underlying all relationships and communities. Some of these negative attitudes are focused on race, gender, sexual orientation, prestige, wealth, physical looks, or special abilities. No matter how subtle, unconscious attitudes can be damaging and divisive within a team. Team members must take personal responsibility for eliminating negative thoughts and feelings from their attitudes. Only in this way will interactions and shared jobs remain positive and clear.

Avoid assumptions.

Assumptions are common when it comes to disability, and the truth is: they're usually wrong! Assumptions are made because it's easier to decide why someone acted in a certain way, rather than asking them personally to explain. Even if the assumption is on the right track, it's hardly ever the full story. Only the person who chose the behavior has all the information on why and how and what. Making an assumption can often begin a snowball of misunderstanding.

Obstacles Will Arise

A good rule of thumb is to expect obstacles! Then they won't seem insurmountable or unwanted. "Oh, so here's the first one. It's not even so bad!" Actually, obstacles will only be experienced as negative if that is the team's reaction to them. They can either be seen as part of the process, or else as interruptions that have to be eliminated. It's helpful to maintain an element of humor if the obstacles start mounting up, remembering that it's the rocks in the river that make such beautiful waves and currents. As in a river, some of the obstacles are boulder-sized, and some are more like pebbles. Some problems may mask others, and even pebbles can gather into a significant hill. Some of the external difficulties that are common to projects stem from:

1. lack of organization: is someone keeping track of due dates, who's responsible for what job, paperwork, record-keeping, and correspondence?

2. financial deficiencies: are there adequate funds for materials, or to pay for professional assistance as needed?

3. interpersonal discomfort or antagonism: are there undercurrents within the team that need to be addressed?

4. lack of administrative support: is the school leadership behind the project, financially and conceptually?

Any good-sized project will have many facets: jobs, meetings, communication, fund-raising, people-coordinating. All of the needs and details can pile up, burying the most enjoyable aspects of the project beneath worry and frustration, making stress the number one obstacle. External obstacles are actually easier to deal with than a high stress level among team members. Even if everything is flowing smoothly on the surface, internal tension can undermine the team's ability to function, and create other very real problems. Unconscious stress, by its very nature, seems to invite crises.

Periodically, a project passes through critical points, when several pressing deadlines arrive simultaneously. A project seems to accelerate as it nears completion. Excitement builds, with the potential of turning into panic. Team members may feel overwhelmed, believing that the project will fail. This type of negativity, which is understandable when one looks at the circumstances, can be deeply upsetting to the project as a whole. Keeping cool is one of the most important goals for the team, as well as taking the time to reassure each other that everything will work out. A clear and relaxed mind is the most likely to come up with good solutions, and laughter is an excellent relief for tension.

Another serious obstacle to inclusion projects is negative reactions from outside sources. Any time an effort is made to change the status quo, reactions can be harsh and extreme. Parents of students with disability may not be keen on the idea of involving their child in a potentially challenging situation. Coming from years of ridicule and separation, they cannot believe that their son or daughter will find welcome in a classroom of general education students. They may not want to take that chance. Other teachers, administrators, or community members may feel that the project could reflect badly on their professional image. Confronting long-hidden ·attitudes is bound to stir up discomfort. Team members may be the ones to receive criticism. The most worthy efforts may be misinterpreted, and teachers who are sincerely trying to bring about real social change in the school may end up accused of exploiting students with disability for their own personal glory. This type of situation is not new, but is a very substantial obstacle.

When Things Go Wrong

Learning about solving conflicts is one of the most educational aspects of teamwork. This is an area of growing interest in schools, families, and government, that unfortunately has not received adequate attention in the past. Daily headlines about war, broken treaties, domestic violence, and criminal youth, point to the need for creative communication skills that effectively address problems. Successful negotiations, where all sides feel acknowledged and satisfied, have been the exception to the rule. Most people want to avoid problems at all cost, even to the extent of pretending they don't exist until everything suddenly falls apart. In retrospect, problems usually make up the instructional, valuable part of life. They force people to change, to be creative in finding new solutions or approaches. Learning to navigate through the challenges of teamwork can be one of the most worthwhile parts of any project. And the interpersonal transformations benefit not only the project, but especially each individual who is conscientious and open to the process. So don't quit before you begin, dreading the problems that lurk in the future! Most teams come through the rough waters intact and wiser, having learned new skills for resolving problems and overcoming obstacles.

Conflict resolution refers to solving a problem between two sides, without either side feeling defeated or ignored. To accomplish this goal usually means taking enough time to hear out both sides, instead of issuing an authoritative command just to settle things quickly. One thing is certain: a conflict does not disappear on its own. If attention is given to the situation, resolution can almost surely be reached. There is a wealth of information about conflict resolution in current books and articles. Ask a local librarian to suggest titles on this subject. Also, see Recommended Resources in the appendix section.

Listed below are some ideas on the essential elements of conflict resolution and for improving communication skills in general. None of them is guaranteed to succeed all of the time. Some will apply to your group more than others. Some will feel more difficult than others. Seek out community professionals who can help guide your team as you learn new ways to communicate. Relief is possible, even for the most uncomfortable, unacceptable positions. Any one person may not know the way out, but someone, somewhere, does. Put your heads together, ask for help, and you're on your way to the next step.

Listening

One of the most common complaints in any argument or discussion is that people do not feel listened to, or adequately heard. We think four times faster than we speak, which means that much of the time someone is talking, the other person is not fully listening. Instead, the other person is thinking, mentally preparing an argument, story, or viewpoint to present when it is his or her time to speak. Most dialogues that address a problem go in circles, with each person talking, talking, talking, and no one truly listening. In such situations, it's a wonder when solutions are reached.

Listening does not mean agreeing! Listening means really trying to get in the other person's shoes for a space of time, to understand how that person sees the situation. This is more difficult than one would think, because it can feel like listening is agreeing. Instead of responding with, "But...," one just listens. Neutral responses include "Yes, I see...okay...go on...I hear what you're saying...yes, I understand..." To put aside one's opinion and perspective temporarily, and just listen to another, enhances the ability to see another point of view. The other perspective may not be convincing, but it often has some aspect of truth that needs to be considered and incorporated into the solution. A solution must be broad enough to hold all parties' needs, and without hearing out those needs, the proper answer cannot be found.

Active listening and reflective listening are two terms for ways to increase listening skills. They refer to the act of repeating back to the speaker certain key elements of what is being said, in order to demonstrate what has been heard. At first, this method can feel unnatural or silly, but it brings excellent results and truly acknowledges the speaker. Active or reflective listening responses include: "So you think that...I hear that you felt hurt when...You believe you weren't treated well because..." Active listening can also include asking the speaker to clarify what was said, to ensure proper understanding. "Can you explain what you mean?...Is this the problem as you see it now?...What do you feel you need in this situation?"

When a speaker is boring, or not making sense, if the vocabulary used is complex beyond understanding, if the speaker is presenting opinions that are offensive to others, or critical, the immediate, almost unconscious reaction is to stop listening. This kind of situation can take a real effort to overcome, in order to continue listening. Cutting the speaker off, or being rude in any way, will only reinforce the lack of communication. Only by staying with the process will one be prepared for a constructive response, rather than a defensive or angry reply. You might ask, "Why bother?" It's true that some people are very difficult to work with, because their manner of communicating seems offensive and uncaring. It seems they will never be able to join with others successfully. Consider that their choice of delivery may be conditioned by years of rejection and criticism from others. They have learned to entrench themselves in their own opinion, and not be budged. Being listened to, with respect, not being rushed or interrupted, is a rare treat for anyone. For some, it can be life-changing. On the other hand, taking the time to listen to others is an experience most people have neglected. Asking questions, clarifying meanings, reflecting back with no judgment or alteration, can be eye-opening and quite refreshing. It's the best way to get to know someone.

Body language is another skill for effective listening. Being aware of one's body language can actually help to focus attention on the speaker, and create a level of interest in what is being said. Attentive listening is demonstrated by facing the person speaking, keeping one's hands at rest in a relaxed position, putting aside any items to be played with or handled, making eye contact, and occasionally nodding one's head. This may seem contrived at first, but it's actually just learning a new skill. After a while, these attitudes will feel comfortable and sincere. Crossed arms, downward eyes, fidgeting with hair or fingernails, taking notes, whispering to someone, or looking out the window, are all examples of distracting behaviors that communicate a lack of interest and attention.

Honesty

Honesty is a quality that can actually be quite scary in many situations. Honesty reveals who we really are, and most social interaction is based on a less intimate level that presents a kind of facade rather than the deepest, truest feelings. Because of this more superficial level of social communication, many people have never learned how to identify their own feelings about a situation, and the best that comes out is a comment aimed at another person. The intention is true, but the effect is hurtful.

A good place to begin learning how to be honest without being hurtful is with "I-messages." This phrase refers to statements that begin with the word "I," in order to communicate feelings instead of opinions about another person. When a situation has stirred emotions, the automatic reaction is to make a "You-message;" for example "You never call me anymore." To rephrase this sentence as an I-message, one would say, "I've been feeling sad that you haven't called me." The level of honesty is apparent immediately. In the you-message, the speaker's true feelings are not even mentioned. In the I-message, the speaker's feelings are the main issue. One reason this approach can be challenging is because it exposes the speaker's deeper self to another.

Will that other person be caring? Will he or she turn the information against the speaker? Does the speaker feel needy or weak because his or her feelings are hurt by being neglected?

Learning to use I-messages takes some practice. Many people think they are using I-messages, when they are actually disguising you-messages: "I feel that you're not being cooperative." Notice how that statement is not about the speaker at all. It does not identify a feeling; it states an opinion about the other person's behavior. A true I-message would be more like this: "I feel afraid that too much responsibility is going to fall on me when I see you not willing to cooperate." This approach focuses on the speaker's fear that is brought up by the other person's actions. I-messages are not just changing the words, but must change the perspective, putting energy into looking at ourselves instead of at others. Take some time to think about what you really want to communicate, before jumping into an I-message. Practice shifting your perspective to see what you actually need or want from a given situation—why it isn't working for you—instead of focusing on what another person is not doing.

Honesty in a team situation requires sensitivity to know what degree of intimacy is appropriate. One cannot go around sharing deep life secrets and experiences with others just because they are on the same team. Using I-messages is a great tool for approaching difficult subjects, but remember to keep it to the point of the work at hand. This is not an arena for therapy. The goal is to find solutions that promote healthy, enjoyable working relationships within the team.

Majority Rule and Consensus

There are two basic methods for settling a disagreement or making a decision within a team. The more familiar is majority rule, in which a vote is taken and a decision is made based on the wishes of a majority of people involved. This method is used commonly in political elections, family decisions, playground games, corporate offices and public referendums, because it is a fairly simple and straightforward method. The majority of people agree to the idea of majority rule. However, it does not necessarily provide the most satisfactory results, as the minority is virtually left out of the solution. They may accept that another solution has been chosen by the greater part of the group, but this cannot fully appease the fact that their alternative was not chosen. Majority rule creates winners and losers, and while it seems to have worked for many, many centuries throughout history, perhaps it has only worked well enough.

An alternative to majority rule is consensus. Consensus means everyone agrees, on some level, to the solution. At first that would seem impossible to accomplish. It does take a greater effort, based on the belief that everyone has the right to be heard, respected, and satisfied as much as possible. With consensus everybody wins, even if nobody ends up with the exact solution desired. But it will be a solution everyone can live with, because everyone contributed a part of it.

In a nutshell, consensus is reached by taking a proposed solution (usually acceptable to the majority) and finding out where and how it does not satisfy some members. Then alternate solutions are drafted, making small changes toward meeting the minority's needs. The original proposal is stretched little by little until it has bridged the gap between differing viewpoints. Each new proposal is discussed and accepted by all or returned to the work table for further revision.

Consensus creates unity because everyone has to sacrifice a little of the personal to ensure that all members are included, and all needs are addressed. Truly workable solutions must arise from the unity of the team, or those feeling left out or unrecognized will find it hard to support the plan. The drawback to consensus is that it takes time, much more than a simple hand-raising vote. Solutions usually need to be hammered out carefully, adjusting details one by one to stay as close as possible to the majority decision, while incorporating the concepts requested by the minority. Consensus is highly recommended as the least divisive, and most unifying, method of problem solving. It takes practice and patience, but is well worth the effort expended. Resources for additional information on this topic can be found in the appendix section at the end of the book.

Flexibility

The attribute of flexibility applies to the team as a whole, as well as to the individual members. The team must be flexible when it comes to plans for the project. The members decide on all the particulars, then adjust that plan as the process unfolds. Even when the plan has seemed so solid and easy, there are times when it must be changed. Outside forces are beyond the control of the group, such as changes in students' and/or team members' lives or schedules, or a redefining of project purpose. Often nothing can be done to maintain the original plan, and the best choice is to "change horses in midstream."

Making major changes once the project has begun demands flexibility of the team members. The team will only be as flexible and adaptable as its individual members. Each person is responsible for working together with the others, being supportive during transition times, and avoiding stubbornness. Digging one's heels into the ground because of a resistance to change will affect the success of the entire project. Flexibility of team members also means commitment to accepting others' opinions, efforts, and ideas. It means letting people be who they are, knowing that any one person, whether it's yourself or another, is never fully in control. Some may want to be, others may appear to be, but the strength of a flexible group will supersede any tyrannical tendencies that may occur.

A good image for the benefits of flexibility is that of a strong, old tree. The strength of the trunk allows the branches to bend and bow in the wind. If the tree were stiff and rigid, it would crack and split under the pressure of the wind. It's better to bend—to circumstances or to another person—rather than break because of resistance.

Outside Mediation

In cases of extreme conflict, a very effective solution is to invite an outside mediator to come work with the team. This person can help open communication in new ways, encourage better listening skills on all sides, and assist in developing the first steps toward a solution. The mediator should be a professional in the field of mediation or psychology, with experience in group work. Preferably the individual will not be allied with one of the team members. It is very important that every member feel positive about the assistance. Otherwise, there may be subconscious resistance to receiving the help which is offered. Everyone must get a chance to be heard and acknowledged. However, if there are members who are stubbornly opposed to outside help, the team may decide to take that direction nonetheless. If the mediator is creative, he or she might be able to involve the members who were holding back. It's always worth a try.

How the mediator facilitates the sessions will be different in each case. There are many innovative techniques to improve group functioning, and they can be fun as well. It helps to remember that the group began with a sense of unity, and somewhere along the way, that sense was lost. The goal of mediation is to restore the unity and enjoyment of the members with each other, and their ability to side-step disagreements and personality difficulties in honor of project goals.

Fun

Personal care is essential to a healthy team, and should probably be first on the list rather than last! How easily we forget to have fun in the midst of responsibilities, deadlines, telephone calls, and all the other organizational details. Sometimes a personal limit is reached, and a member has to take a break in order to recover a relaxed attitude about the project. Unfortunately, most organizations do not honor this essential need for personal "off" time. The result is burnout, a term that most teachers are familiar with, given the weighty workload in today's public school systems: class prep, grading, extracurricular activities, personal time with students, administrative demands, continuing education requirements, etc. Bureaucracies by nature cannot encourage individual care; they are designed to function as a well-oiled machine, and each person must carry the load daily. There is just not time for breaks and pauses. Participating in an inclusion project will also be another responsibility to carry. Even the most energetic people eventually reach a limit, and need to do things differently. When adequate personal care is lacking, team members can get edgy, impatient, rigid and controlling.

Remember to schedule fun activities for yourself and as a team. Each person knows what he or she enjoys doing, something that is completely unrelated to school, projects or work. It may take a dedicated effort to set aside a time free from all thoughts of lists and deadlines. Sports, time with children or pets, exercise, reading, cooking a special meal, visiting with friends, art work, or writing are some of the numerous possibilities for activities that reduce stress. The most important feature of the activity is that is should not be pressured. The objective is to relieve pressure, so it must be fun.

For the team as a whole, here are a few suggestions for ways to incorporate fun into meetings, and to support each other in making time for fun.

• At a team meeting, have all members list five activities that help them relax and forget about the stresses in their lives.

• Have lunch together, either brown bag or eating out.

• Every week, one team member reports on what he or she did for fun that week.

• Schedule meetings in a park, a coffee house, or someone's home, instead of always at school.

And a Bit of Luck

Sad to say, successful teams are the exception to the rule! Our society is primarily oriented to individual achievement, competition, and control. Shared leadership has few current role models; interdependence is a concept just recently rising on the horizon. This doesn't mean your efforts are doomed from the start. On the contrary, teamwork can produce one of the best feelings in the world, even for brief moments of integrated, smooth functioning. No matter how difficult it gets, there is always a time frame; in other words, it won't last forever. The worst scenario is that you get through it as best you can and then it's over; you don't have to deal with this or that person for a while, if ever again!

Every team is learning for and with the rest. Your efforts will contribute to the next team, and theirs to the next, and so on. Creativity and commitment will lead to new ways to communicate and overcome personality barriers. Discomfort evolves into acceptance, for people with and without disability. Teamwork is educational in the truest sense: plan to let go of expectations, plan to be frustrated, plan to see beyond obstacles and difficulties. Put effort into having fun, getting to know other team members and yourself, and pulling off a project that reflects your highest ideals. Ask for help from those who have skills in polishing a group's interaction. With a bit of luck, belief in the process, and a lot of heart, you'll be following in the footsteps of our country's Olympic teams: *Go for the gold!*

Myths and Misconceptions

All children with Down's Syndrome are pure love.

This misconception is a stereotype of both children and adults with Down's Syndrome. While many of these individuals exhibit a childlike innocence and love, they are also individual people with personalities and characteristics that vary from one to another. People with Down's Syndrome can be angry, stubborn, frustrated, and sad at times, despite a general demeanor of open affection.

People with disability usually cannot find employment.

More and more, it's becoming a recognized fact that workplace inaccessibility is more of a barrier to employment than a person's disability. As our country improves transportation and architectural accessibility, the work force is increasing its numbers of skilled people with disability.

Anyone that cannot speak clearly is not intelligent.

Speech and intelligence are two separate areas of ability. Speech impairment does not indicate a particular level of intelligence. Many people with above average intelligence have difficulty speaking, and may even need to use computer-synthesized voice assistance.

Learning disability only affects a child's performance in the classroom.

Learning disability can affect more than school performance. A child may be frustrated by the inability to communicate on the same level with his or her peers. For a child with this type of disability, feeling inferior or misunderstood in social interactions, self-expression, joking, and wittiness can lead to negative behaviors on the playground or in the classroom.

A child with a severe hearing loss cannot learn to speak.

Contrary to this common belief, many people with hearing loss can lip-read and speak. They are able to learn how to form words and make sounds well enough to be understood by others. These techniques are often taught in conjunction with sign language, to enable those with hearing impairments the greatest range of communication possible.

Aware of Our Words and Actions

Inappropriate:	"Will your child ever be normal?"
	"He is a mongoloid child."
	"One of my students is a midget."
	Offering money to an adult or child (stranger) with disability.
Appropriate:	"What is the prognosis for your child's disability?"
	"He has Down's Syndrome."
	"One of my students is very short, about three feet in height."
	Saying hello to a stranger with disability, or asking if you can be of help.

Ideas for Discussion

1. Elements of a successful team

Most students are avid fans of one or more sports teams, and will be happy to talk about their knowledge and understanding of how a team functions. Have they ever looked at potential pitfalls in teamwork? Have students recall their own experiences on teams. Any horror stories? What made teamwork challenging for them? What made it fun? Do they enjoy working with others, or do they prefer individual sports such as bike riding, skiing, swimming, or roller-blading? What are the pros and cons of working in a team, and working individually? Use information from the sections above to initiate discussion about issues of communication, flexibility, leadership, commitment, and unity.

How is a classroom like a team? A family? A group of friends? How does leadership fluctuate and shift from one person to another within these groups? Discuss variations in structure. Some students prefer less guidance, with a more self-determined structure. Others enjoy stricter guidance by the teacher or leader. How could these differences cause problems within a team? How might the problems be remedied?

2. Barriers of prejudice

Prejudice exists in many subtle forms, even within a school population. Discussion about prejudice, what it is, how it forms, the problems it causes, and how it can be transformed, applies directly to the initial stages of building a team of students comprised of those with and those without disability. Compare different groupings that occur within a student body, and some of the negative names associated with each: students that participate in sports (jocks), students with high academic priorities (nerds), students with alternative sexual orientation (queers, fags), students with alternative life styles (hippies, stoners), students with communication and learning differences (retards). Prejudice also exists around multicultural and ethnic differences. Open the discussion for honest examination of how students identify, separate, and judge members of these various groupings. Ask students how it feels to be put in a category and judged according to that group. How does it feel to make that kind of judgment about another student? Have any of the students experienced having a prejudice dismantled by personally meeting someone who was previously labeled or judged, and finding that the person was not at all like anticipated? Continue the discussion relating it to team building. How do these attitudes get in the way of working together? How do assumptions limit one's ability to hear another point of view?

Lesson Plans

Photo Pages

See Lesson Plans in Chapter 2 for guidelines to using the photo pages for this chapter.

Council Circle (grades 4 - 12)

Objective: to introduce students to a method of conflict resolution dating back to ancient times; to encourage listening skills with the intention of appreciating others' perspectives; to increase verbal self-expression.

Timeframe: one or more class periods.

Steps:

1. Have students arrange their chairs in a large circle, so that each student can see every other student.

2. Explain the process of council circle: This is a method of sharing, listening, getting to know each other, and settling a disagreement when needed. Members sit in a circle to show that no one comes before anyone else; each member is of equal value. The most important points are to speak from the heart, and to listen with full attention to the speaker. What is being said must be respected and not ridiculed. The group must agree that this will be a safe place to share, and to be honest. A talking piece, which is any object such as a small stone, is passed around the circle. Only the person with the talking piece may speak. Others must listen until it is their turn. When the speaker has finished, the talking piece is handed to the next person in the circle. It is always acceptable to pass, sitting a few moments in silence or passing the piece as soon as one wishes. This process has been used throughout history, by Native Americans and other indigenous peoples, to strengthen the group and to share each member's point of view in a safe way.

3. Review the rules of a council circle. You may want to make a poster listing the rules, to be visible during the council.

• Only the person with the talking piece may speak. Others listen respectfully to each speaker until their turn to speak.

• Speak in response to the topic. Don't take more than your appropriate time. Some groups may want to use a timer to make sure everyone gets a turn to speak.

• Speak about yourself, using I-messages. Do not answer someone else's question, give advice, or comment about what was said by another.

• Speak about your thoughts, experiences, feelings, and ideas. It's okay to talk about something that hurt your feelings, or made you feel good.

• You don't have to plan ahead what you will say. Sometimes it's best to wait until your turn, and then speak spontaneously about the topic.

• Everything that is said in the circle must be kept within the group. This is called confidentiality, and it means that all members are safe to share, knowing that what is said will not be repeated to others outside the circle, or used against them later.

• The leader (teacher) has the role of making sure that any hurtful speaking is interrupted and redirected. This is the only time when interruption or cross-speaking is allowed.

4. Present the topic. For a beginning council circle, the topic should not be overly intimate or personal. Possible suggestions for beginning councils include: Tell about your family's background (family traditions and celebrations, family values, ethnic heritage). Tell a story about a time when you were very scared. Tell the group about a person who has influenced or changed your life (a friend, relative, or someone you have never met but know about through the news or books). Tell a story about a pet or animal that you had or that you knew. Share a dream you had (if you don't remember a dream, you can tell a story about something interesting or funny that happened to you). If you could be anyone else in the world, who would you be, and why? Tell what you know about your name (first, last, or middle): how did you get it, who gave it to you, what does it mean?

5. After the talking piece has passed around the circle one time, ask if any of the members who chose to pass would like to speak now. When everyone has had one opportunity to speak, introduce a second topic to close the circle. A good topic for this part is to ask, "What was your response to speaking in this way in a council circle?" Some students will probably comment on how different it feels to have the undivided attention of a group of listeners; this is a rare experience for most. Others may have felt nervous.

6. The teacher may explain to the group that this is a new format for communicating, and there may be some adjustment. At first it may feel a little uncomfortable. Afterwards, you might notice that you feel good, like you got to say what you really wanted to, and that others really listened.

7. If the group wants to continue exploring council circles, advanced topics will move into more personal issues, such as prejudice, labeling of groups or individuals, dreams and aspirations, fears and anxieties, experiences in family relationships and friendship.

Student Court (grades 4–12)

Objective: to develop mediation skills in students.
Timeframe: periodic throughout a semester or school year.
Steps:
1. Set up an alternating "court" of three or five students. Each month the court members will change.

2. When there is a discipline problem or other conflict within the classroom, the teacher decides if it is an appropriate situation to refer to the court. Students bring complaints to the teacher, who will delegate to the court whenever appropriate. The teacher can also bring complaints directly to the court. The teacher may wish to retain the final authority in a conflict, but ask for recommendations from the court. In other situations, the teacher may give the court full authority to make a final decision.

3. The court may meet during class time in front of the class, as in a real courtroom. In this event, the class may not make comments or interrupt the proceedings, just as in an actual courtroom proceeding.

4. The petitioner(s) presents the case, and asks for a decision. The court members must decide how to handle the situation, and what types of conflict resolution methods will be used. The court may request that the students and/or teacher involved in the conflict have a mediated discussion in front of the court. Rules of no cross-talking, demonstrated active listening, and I-messages are in effect, monitored and guided by the court members. Court members must pay particular attention to ensure respect and cooperation in the discussion.

5. The court may withdraw to a separate space to make a decision, or have its own decision-making discussion in front of the class (same rules apply). When making a ruling, the court members should strive for consensus, practice active listening skills with each other, and propose/adjust creative solutions. If the court cannot reach consensus after a reasonable period of time, it can resort to a majority vote.

6. The court has authority to determine disciplinary action, such as: loss of recess time; extra class duties; making apologies, written or verbal; or other appropriate consequences.

7. The classroom teacher always maintains the authority to remove the conflict from the court and take action personally.

Student Biography: Felicia

7.1: Felicia

Felicia is nineteen years old, and has a disability called cerebral palsy, or C.P. Cerebral palsy is a very common disability, which results from brain damage around the time of a child's birth. Something happens in the brain which causes brain cells to die. Since the brain controls all functions of the body, any damage in the brain

Figure 7.1 Felicia (photo by Ted Schooley).

will cause a part of the body to stop working or to only work partial-ly. In Felicia's case, her arms and legs were affected, and also her voice. Felicia's mother was very young when Felicia was born, about 17 years old. There is more chance of a teenage mother having a child with a disability, than there is for an adult mother whose body has completed its development.

Felicia has a sparkly enthusiasm for life. Most of the time she is smil-ing. She enjoys being with people, caring for her pets, doing different projects, and reading teen magazines. Since she can't speak, Felicia uses her face, eyes, and hands to express her feelings. People that spend time with Felicia–her friends, family, and teachers–are able to understand what she is saying or asking. She's very aware of all that is going on around her, and has no problem following her high school schedules every day. Without words, you can tell if Felicia is happy, sad, silly, serious, or angry.

Questions:

1. Why do you think Felicia's C.P. is considered moderate? How might a mild form of cerebral palsy look? What about a severe case?

2. What would it be like to understand everything around you but not be able to join in by talking?

3. Do you think most teenagers know that there is a higher chance of having a baby with disability if they get pregnant?

7.2: Writing

The left side of Felicia's body is weaker than the right side, due to the brain damage. This makes her walking uneven, and one hand doesn't work well. In this photo you can see that she is writing. Because her fingers are always in a closed position, it helps her hold onto the pencil.

The most difficult social problem for Felicia is her drooling, which you can see in the picture. The disability makes her unable to close her mouth. Everyone makes saliva, and we swallow when our mouths have too much. Think how many times each day you swallow, with-out even thinking about it. Felicia can't do that, so the saliva comes out. She wears a bandanna around her neck, and uses it to wipe her mouth regularly. She does exercises to help strengthen her mouth muscles.

Figure 7.2 Writing (photo by Bill Davis).

Felicia is very sensitive, which sometimes makes it hard for her, having a disability. So many students are actually afraid of people with disabilities, and they avoid kids like Felicia. She is very aware that the drooling bothers people and causes them to stare at her. It doesn't seem fair that she gets rejected for something she can't control. Because she is very social and fun-loving, she doesn't like to be left out. But not being able to talk makes it hard for her to make new friends. Luckily, she has good friends in her special ed class, who also have disabilities and understand her feelings. With them, she can openly share her laughter and playful personality. But sometimes she wishes she were like all the other students, as she stands in the doorway of her class and watches the kids walk by in the hall.

Questions:

1. What do you do if one of your friends starts drooling?
2. What might Felicia be thinking as she watches the students walk by her class?
3. How could people help make Felicia feel more comfortable about her disability?

7.3: The Voice

Felicia has a special computer into which she can type words and it "speaks" out loud for her. It's called her "Voice." She doesn't use it at home, because her parents can understand her hand gestures and facial expressions. Other people have a harder time understanding, and it can be very frustrating for Felicia when she wants to communicate. Understanding Feilcia takes a lot, but she has a beautiful smile that she gives to those who make the effort. Having the Voice helps her talk with people who don't know her well enough to understand her signs and sounds.

Figure 7.3 The Voice (photo by Bob Blair).

When Felicia first got the Voice, the teachers soon found that the computer's memory was almost full. They thought something was wrong with it, and were about to send it back, when Felicia finally told them that she was keeping a personal journal in the Voice. She had figured out how to program the journal files so that no one else could get into them—just like a diary with a lock on it!

Most of Felicia's friends are classmates who have been in school with her for years. You may be surprised to know that sometimes she calls them on the phone at night. They ask questions, and she answers by making sounds. They ask questions until they understand what she wants. She loves to dance, and is going to the prom with her class.

Questions:

1. What would it be like to call someone on the phone if you couldn't speak? How would your friends know it was you?

2. What would it be like to dance in front of other people when you have a disability that makes your body move awkwardly?

3. In what ways does the voice computer change Felicia's life?

7.4: Walking with a Friend

Felicia's cerebral palsy is considered moderate, which means it falls mid-way between mild disability and severe disability. She can walk, her hearing is fine, and she can understand everything going on around her. Sometimes she needs to hold onto someone's arm while walking, if the ground is uneven or steep. Felicia cannot talk at all, but she has a great laugh!

Felicia spends part of her school day in the special ed classroom, but also goes to several general ed classes each day. She likes doing different things in school. She learns practical skills in school, along with simple academics. Last year, Felicia starred in a school play about disability. Of course, she didn't speak any lines, but used sign language for her part. Since she only uses one hand, Felicia's sign language is her own personal style. Anyone who learns her signs can understand her. The signs she uses are very similar to the regular signs, just a little different.

She is kind and caring, comforting people when they are sad. She laughs hard and loud at jokes, and is fun to be with. On the other hand, there are times when she gets very angry, stomping out of the room and staying away until she has calmed down. What causes Felicia's anger? Usually frustration over not being able to use her hands better, or not being able to do her math work.

Figure 7.4 Walking with a Friend (photo by Bill Davis).

Questions:

1. What kinds of things would make you frustrated or angry if you had a disability like Felicia's?

2. Do you think people with disabilities also get frustrated over the same things you do?

3. What are the benefits for Felicia being in the special ed class? What are the benefits for her being in general ed classes?

7.5: Rolling Around

Felicia enjoys going to the movies with her mom, and watching television. She understands everything going on. She rarely needs help, and is able to prepare simple foods, wash the dishes, bathe and dress herself, carry things, and do laundry. She would like to have her own apartment some day, and get a job, maybe as a secretary since she can type, or as a daycare worker with small children. Many people with disabilities like Felicia's live in group houses where they help each other.

Figure 7.5 Rolling Around (photo by Bill Davis).

Felicia can take part in many fun activities, and wishes she was included more with other students. As a teenager, it's very hard for her, because she wants so much to meet boys and go on dates. But boys and girls get to know each other mostly through talking, and Felicia can't do that. It takes a lot of time and effort to communicate with her. Also, many students still feel uncomfortable around someone with a disability, and don't want to be friends.

In the photo, Felicia is getting physical therapy to keep her muscles loose. This helps prevent muscle spasms, which sometimes make her arms or legs jerk out of control. Obviously, she's having a great time rolling back and forth on the log pillow.

Questions:

1. Which do you think is harder: being a young child with a disability, being a teenager with a disability, or being an adult with a disability? Explain your answer.

2. If you were an office manager, how would you feel about hiring someone like Felicia, knowing she would type and file more slowly than someone without a disability?

APPENDIX

A REAL-LIFE INCLUSION PROJECT

Project-based inclusion is not just a "good idea." It has been substantiated by years of practice and refinement. Following is a description of a recent project successfully completed by two high school classes. The general ed class was a Culture and Folk Art class whose curriculum included study of different cultures. The special ed class was comprised of students with moderate to severe disability: some used wheelchairs, some could walk but not very well, some could not talk, some were very verbal and mobile, some were mobile but lacked cognitive awareness, etc. It was a mixed array of students, and at the onset most of them—in both classes—were nervous.

The project centered around the production of a play using student actors and large puppets made by the classes. Presented to both school and public audiences, the play addressed issues of disability awareness on a level that would be appropriate for all ages. Timeframe was approximately five months. A sideline project involved having a high school senior make a documentary film about the entire project, in order to share the process with other schools (see Recommended Resources for information on *Can You Hear Me*, the project documentary and *The Kids Next Door*, a tape of the project's theater production).

The first two months were spent preparing the classes according to the eight-week plan outlined in Chaper 6. Educational speakers and joint class activities were arranged for every week. The classes began getting used to each other. A professional puppeteer was contracted to make puppets with the students. Plaster of Paris heads were shaped onto long dowels; hands were formed. Once the play was roughed in, the characters were dressed and painted as the famous people they would represent: Ludwig von Beethoven, Ray Charles, Franklin Roosevelt, and Katharine Hepburn. The puppet-making proved to be an excellent shared activity for students with and without disability. Some jobs, such as advertisement sales and program design, were handled solely by general ed students. But fun activities, educational lessons and speakers continued throughout the project time. Sessions on sign language, xenophobia (fear of different cultures), sensitivity trainings, and discussions on various topics kept the focus on disability. Student/teacher participation on a radio talk show, and newspaper coverage as part of a series of articles on the district special ed department, provided effective publicity for the play. Two public showings brought in full audiences.

201

While the project was enormously successful, and impacted a large segment of the community, including parents, friends, business sponsors, school board and administrators, and general audience, there were also a number of accompanying problems, as can be expected with any project of this magnitude. Not all students were as open and responsive as others; not everyone changed attitudes within the timeframe of the project. An occasional student would make a degrading comment toward a classmate with disability, which was usually responded to by team leaders. The actors who had to depict prejudice and mockery had a very difficult time acting out those scenes, and much discussion took place about why it was okay in this particular context, that is, to educate people. Personality conflicts within the team rose and fell; funding appeared to be seriously lacking until the last minute; students with leading roles were not showing up for rehearsals; parents were not showing up to pick up their children! Somehow, the pieces fell into place, and the final product was professional and enjoyable. Prior projects that were similar in scope had prepared the team leaders for possible pitfalls and danger areas. Much was learned that will not be repeated in the future, and much was learned that will be retained forever.

SPECIAL NEEDS CHECKLIST

Elements to be Aware of in the Learning Environment:

- Physical accessibility: an environment where students can manage and control as many of their needs as possible.
- Rest: observe students' fatigue patterns and adjust the activity schedule accordingly.
- Teasing or name-calling: address incidents as they occur. Promote discussion on the hurtfulness of name-calling.
- Attention-keeping: use student's name, make eye contact, repeat instructions patiently.
- Information: prepare the students for transitions.
- Pace setting: adjust schedules to address students' needs.
- Autonomy: encourage student-chosen activities when possible
- Respect: honor the need for privacy and personal care time.
- Emotional needs: be sensitive to situations that cause students to feel anxiety or shame.

FAMOUS PEOPLE WITH DISABILITY

The following list identifies some famous people and their disability. This can be used as a quiz game, mix and match, or for suggestions for research papers or biographies.

Sarah Bernhardt: French actress, who continued her acting career after a leg amputation.

Ludwig von Beethoven: Austrian composer who was deaf when he composed his 9th Symphony.

Thomas Edison: Inventor of electricity, had a learning disability that prevented him from reading until he was twelve years old. He continued having a (difficulty with) writing even when he was older.

Albert Einstein: Mathematician/physicist, did not speak until age 4. Because of his learning disability, he had a very difficult time with math in school.

Stephen Hawking: Mathematician/physicist, has Lou Gehrig's disease, a degenerative disease of the nervous system. He uses a wheelchair and speaks with a voice synthesizer.

John Milton: English author/poet became blind at age 43, after which time he wrote Paradise Lost.

Franklin Roosevelt: U.S. President, at age 39, his legs became paralyzed from polio. He was the only president to be elected to office for four terms.

Harriet Tubman: Slavery abolitionist, In childhood, she was hit on the head by a slave overseer, and sustained a skull fracture. The injury resulted in narcolepsy, a condition where one falls asleep spontaneously. She rescued hundreds of slaves on the underground railroad.

Christopher Reeves: Movie actor, paralyzed from the neck down after falling from a horse, he uses a motorized wheelchair while he continues to direct movies. He starred in the movie *Superman.*

Katherine Hepburn: Oscar-winning movie actress who developed Parkinson's Disease.

Homer: Greek poet from the 8th century B.C. who was blind. Famous for his epic poems *The Iliad* and *The Odyssey.*

Itzhak Perlman: Concert violinist who is paraplegic.

Richard Pryor: Actor and comedian who developed muscular sclerosis.

Stevie Wonder: Contemporary musician, composer and singer who is blind.

Ray Charles: Contemporary musician, composer and singer who is blind.

Famous people with learning disability:

Walt Disney	Winston Churchill	Nelson Rockefeller
Alexander Graham Bell	General George Patton	George Washington
Woodrow Wilson	Tom Cruise	Whoopi Goldberg
Agatha Christie	John Lennon	Leonardo da Vinci

Famous people with epilepsy:

Julius Caesar	Tchaikovsky	Charles Dickens
Napoleon	Vincent van Gogh	

Famous people with ADHD (related to hyperactivity):

Robin Williams	"Magic" Johnson

FAMOUS PEOPLE CELEBRITY QUIZ

a. Albert Einstein
b. Walt Disney
c. Nelson Rockefeller
d. F.W. Woolworth

e. Winston Churchill
f. Hans Christian Anderson
g. George Patton
h. Tom Cruise

Match the descriptions below with the celebrity letter above.

1. As a child he was labeled as slow. He clerked in a village grocery store. He suggested putting slow-moving merchandise on a counter and selling it for five cents. This venture was so successful that it was continued with new goods. He became the principal founder of a chain of five-and-ten cents stores.

2. When he was 12 years old, he could not read, and he remained deficient in reading all his life. However, he could memorize entire lectures, which is how he got through school. He became a famous general during World War II.

3. He was slow in school work and did not have a successful school experience, but later became a well-known movie producer and cartoonist.

4. This noted Englishman had much difficulty in school. He later became a national leader and an English Prime Minister.

5. This young boy had difficulty reading but was able to write some of the world's best loved stories.

6. This boy could not talk until the age of four. He did not learn to read until he was nine. His teachers considered him to be mentally slow, unsociable, and a dreamer. He failed the entrance exam for college. Ultimately, he developed the theory of relativity.

7. He is a famous movie star. He learns his lines by listening to a tape, since he has problems reading as a result of dyslexia.

8. This person had much difficulty reading as a young man and throughout his life. However, he was the governor of New York for four terms and later won congressional approval to be appointed vice president of the United States.

Answers to Celebrity Quiz
1. d.   2. g.   3. b.   4. e.   5. f.   6. a.   7. h.   8. c.

OVERVIEW OF PRIMARY LEGISLATION AFFECTING STUDENTS WITH DISABILITY

Rehabilitation Act of 1973 - Section 504

Purpose

Section 504 of the Rehabilitation Act of 1973 is a civil rights law which protects the rights of, and prohibits discrimination against, individuals with disability. The law applies to any program receiving federal funding from the Department of Health, Education and Welfare.

Who Qualifies

• Section 504 protects all school-aged children who have a physical or mental impairment which limits a major life activity, or is regarded as disabled by others. The disabling condition need only limit one major life activity in order to qualify a student. Examples of major life activities include: seeing, breathing, walking, learning, working, caring for oneself, and performing manual tasks. Children do not need to qualify under the Individuals with Disabilities Educational Act (1997) to receive the protection of a 504 plan. 504 qualification is considered when a student with disability, who does not qualify for special education services, has one or more of the following criteria present:
  • A student shows a pattern of not benefiting from the instruction being provided.
  • A student is being considered for retention (not passing to the next grade).
  • A student returns to school after a lengthy period because of serious illness or injury.
  • A student returns to school after expulsion or suspension.
  • A student does not qualify for special education services.
  • A student is transferring out of the special education program.
  • A student has a substance abuse problem.
  • A student is at risk for dropping out of school.
  • A student takes medication at school.

The 504 Plan

A 504 Plan provides the following:
• Evaluation by a team of professionals working with the student.
• Development and implementation of a plan that reasonably accommodates the modifications necessary for the student to benefit from an educational program.

• Procedural safeguards for the student and the student's parents.
• Review and reevaluation before any change in placement.

There is no federal funding available to implement Section 504 requirements. Funding is the responsibility of the individual state and district. A student can be eligible for a 504 Plan without qualifying for special education services. Section 504 provides detailed regulations regarding building and program accessibility. School districts employing more than fifteen people must have a 504 coordinator. The coordinator is responsible for assuring district compliance with Section 504 rulings, including a grievance procedure.

Examples of Section 504 Students

• A student with physical disability who has no cognitive impairment and needs accommodations such as accessible desks, water fountains, ramps, electric doors, etc.
• A student with hearing impairment who needs special seating or special amplification devices.
• A student with severe vision impairment who needs a tape recorder or taped materials to complete assignments and follow-up studies at home.

Individuals With Disabilities Educational Act (1997)

(Also known as IDEA-B. The original act (IDEA, 1990) was reauthorized in 1997, and currently determines special education services.)

Purpose

IDEA-B ensures that all students with disability have a free and appropriate public education.

Who Qualifies

IDEA-B applies to all students with disability from birth to age 21. There are specific categories of qualifying conditions for IDEA-B. A team of professionals develop an Individual Education Plan (IEP) that will meet the educational needs of the student. The IEP requires the school district to provide the services identified as necessary by the team.

Main Provisions

• Provision of child-find activities by district to identify eligible children;
• Notification of parental rights;
• Specific notification to parents about identification of students, evaluation results, and placement decisions;

- Written notice to parents for any change of placement;
- Parental consent for initial evaluation and placement;
- Reevaluation of the student's qualifying disability every three years;
- Independent evaluation if requested by parents;
- Provision of due process hearings if a parent or guardian disagrees with the student's identification, placement, or evaluation;
- Provision of related services to students with disability attending private schools;
- Provision of education in the Least Restrictive Environment. The act contains strong language that supports inclusion when appropriate;
- Measurable and observable goals to be identified in the IEP;
- A State Advisory Board to oversee use of the federal funding received by the district.

The IEP Requirements

- Statements addressing a student's present levels of performance;
- Statements addressing how the student's disability affects participation in the general education curriculum;
- Statements regarding the implementation of goals and objectives;
- Statements regarding how a student's progress will be measured;
- Identification of related services to be provided;
- Identification of program modifications necessary for the student to benefit from the educational plan;
- Explanation of the extent, if any, to which the student will not participate with general education students;
- Statement of the assessment that qualifies the student;
- Projected beginning date of services;
- Beginning at age 14, a statement of transition services the student will need, to be updated annually.

Discipline of Students with Disability

- School personnel is allowed to order a change of placement to an alternative setting.
- Students with disability may be placed in an alternative setting if their disability caused the violation of school policy.
- A school cannot suspend or expel a student with disability for more than ten school days per year.
- A behavior intervention plan must be written before or no later than the ten days of suspension.
- A student will not lose related services during a suspension.
- If a student is a danger to him/herself or others, a hearing must take place to determine placement.
- If a disciplinary action is contemplated as a result of drug/alcohol use or injury to self or others, or if a change of placement for more than ten days occurs, a manifest determination hearing must take place.

• A manifest determination hearing decides if the disability caused the behavior.

• In order to determine if the disability did cause the behavior, the team must determine the following:

1. If the IEP and placement were appropriate;

2. If the student's disability impaired his/her ability to understand the consequences of the behavior;

3. If the student's disability impaired the student's ability to control his/her behavior.

> • If it is determined that the disability did not cause the behavior, the student can be disciplined in the same manner as a student without disability.

> • If it is determined that the disability caused the behavior, IDEA-B outlines specific procedures that districts must follow when disciplining the student with disability.

RECOMMENDED RESOURCES

Films

If I Can't Do It, a video production of the life story of Arthur Campbell, Jr., a man with disability who was very active in the disability rights movement. Walter Brock Productions, 812-945-7719.

Can You Hear Me, video documentary of a high school project-based inclusion project. In It Together Productions, 505-751-9491.

Books

Hent, Deborah & Quinlan, Kathryn: *Extraordinary People with Disabilities*, New York: Children's Press, 1996.

Zimmerman, Jack & Coyle, Virginia: *The Way of Council*, Bramble, Las Vegas, 1996.

Fisher, Roger & Ury, William: *Getting to Yes, Negotiating Agreement Without Giving In*, Penguin, New York, 1991.

Vassar Miller (Ed.): *Despite This Flesh: The Disabled in Stories and Poems*, University of Texas Press, Austin, 1985.

National Resources

NICHCY (National Information Center for Children and Youth with Disabilities). This group publishes an extensive listing of toll-free numbers for organizations and agencies serving all disabilities. P.O. Box 1492, Washington, DC, 20013-1492, 800-695-0285, http://www.nichcy.org.

National Public Radio (NPR), 635 Massachusetts Ave., Washington, DC, 20001, 202-414-2000.

NPR recommended programs:

1) *Beyond Affliction: The Disability History Project*, http://www.NPR.org (click on Programs select Talk Shows, select Cultural and Information. This website offers a variety of information beyond the audio program, as well as directions for listening to or ordering tapes and manuscripts.

2) *The Disability Series*, http://www.NPR.org/programs/totn/archives (click on 1998, click on May, select May 4 - 8, 1998. Topics include: Universal design, recreation, assistive technologies.

Classroom Curriculum

Friends Who Care Teachers Kit. Disability awareness curriculum for elementary/middle school grades. Includes a 16-page teachers guide, activity sheet, posters, a 45 min. video tape. National Easter Seal Society, Communications Dept.,

230 West Monroe Street, Suite 1800, Chicago, IL, 60606, 800-221-6827, http://www.seals.com

Just Like Me and You. Disability awareness curriculum materials and ideas for grades 3, 4 and 5, by Paraquad, Inc. a disability organization. Paraquad, Inc., 311 N. Lindbergh, St. Louis, MO, 63141, 314-567-1558, http://www.paraquad.org/dis-aware.htm

Konczal, Dee & Getskow, Veronica: *Kids With Special Needs,* Clark, Kimberly (Ed.), Learning Works, Santa Barbara, 1996. Elementary grades curriculum for disability awareness.

INDEX

Related services: 112-114, 207
Research paper: 136
Resentment: 85, 86
Resource room: 49
Respite care: 79, 80, 81
Responsibilities of educators: 5
Rheumatic fever: 123
Ritalin: 127, 129
Role models for disability: 24-25, 153
Roosevelt, Franklin D.: 25
Rubella: 58

S

Schizophrenia: 120
Scoliosis: 121
Section 504: 4, 110-111, 121, 205-206
Segregation by disability: xv
Seizures: 59, 87
Self-assessment Survey: 32-34, 37-38,
   150, 155, 174
   graphing of: 43-44
Self-contained classroom: 145, 156
Sensitivity training: 100, 133, 150
Seriously emotionally disturbed: 120, 126
Service learning: 146
Sexual behaviors: 88
Sexual issues: 88-89
Shaken baby syndrome: 62, 65
Shame: 28, 37
Sibling issues: 73, 85-86, 89
Sickle cell anemia: 123
Sign language: 197
Skilled nursing: 114
Slang terms for disability: 130
Social issues: 80-82
Social Security: 79, 92
Social work services: 114
Special education: 109-127
   development of: 5
Special needs checklist: 202
Special students: 11, 109-127
Specific learning disabled: 124, 125
Speech and language impairment: 59,
   119, 187
Speech therapy: 113, 121
Spinal cord injury: 61
Sports teams: 171-173, 188-189
Standards of beauty: 22
Stander: 104

Stereotypes: 6, 7, 175-176
Stress: 78, 85, 177
Stroke: 45, 50, 59
Student biographies, about: 10
Student court: 192
Students together: 160-166
Supplemental Security Income (SSI): 79,
   92
Support: 78, 83, 84, 102
   services: 90, 91, 93

T

Talking piece: 190
Teachers, as role models: 29-30
   responsibilities of: 5, 8, 93
Team building, skills: 173-174
   communication: 174, 175, 176, 178, 180
   obstacles to: 177-178
Team work: 77, 112, 149, 167-186
Terminology for disabilities: 134
Thalidomide: 57
Transportation: 90-91, 106
Traumatic brain injury: 61, 122
Tube feeding: 74
Tuberculosis: 123

U

Unconscious attitudes/values: xiii, 23, 27,
   148, 175, 176
Unity: 168-169
Unknown causes: 53, 57, 60

V

Visible disability: 21, 24-25, 127, 175
Victimization: 23
Visual impairment: 59, 118, 129-130
Voice (computerized): 107, 196-197

W

Warning label survey: 67-68
Wheelchair: 13, 16, 20, 25, 43, 78, 100,
   104-105, 121, 130, 164,

X

X-rays: 58

Y

Yoke: 168, 175
You-messages: 181-182

The purpose of this book is to reduce the discomfort and alienation of teachers and students regarding people with disabilities through the use of written and photographic materials. It aims to dispel misconceptions that contribute to stereotyping and in general to blur the divisions between two segments of our society: those with disabilities and those without. *Disability Awareness in the Classroom* provides excellent training for general education teachers and students preparing for inclusion or wanting to enhance their inclusion experiences. Each chapter contains ideas for classroom activities, discussion, and curriculum planning. The separate packet of large 5 1/2" x 8 1/2" photo cards which accompany the book will give readers the opportunity to look at the "differentness" of others without inhibition and without hurting anyone's feelings. Even when a class has had included students in the past, a presentation on acceptance of differences is an invaluable topic and will benefit students not only in the school environment but also in their personal lives. Teachers and students together need to be able to look inquisitively at the differences in others, to identify the similarities, and to ask questions and formulate answers and opinions, and this book will help fill that need.

ISBN 0-398-06953-0

9 780398 069537

Diabetic Sweet Treats

AmMed Direct® / Better Care
1-877-700-3800

Discover more of your favorite recipes!

For additional titles write to:
Favorite All Time Recipes™
7373 N. Cicero Ave.
Lincolnwood, IL 60712

Pictured on the front cover: Chocolate Mint Cups *(page 15).*
Pictured on the back cover *(left to right):* Rich Chocolate Cheesecake *(page 6)* and Honeydew Melon Sorbet *(page 36).*

Nutritional Analysis: Every effort has been made to check the accuracy of the nutritional information that appears with each recipe. However, because numerous variables account for a wide range of values for certain foods, nutritive analyses in this book should be considered approximate. Different results may be obtained by using different nutrient databases and different brand-name products.

Microwave Cooking: Microwave ovens vary in wattage. Use the cooking times as guidelines and check for doneness before adding more time.

Preparation/Cooking Times: Preparation times are based on the approximate amount of time required to assemble the recipe before cooking, baking, chilling or serving. These times include preparation steps such as measuring, chopping and mixing. The fact that some preparations and cooking can be done simultaneously is taken into account. Preparation of optional ingredients and serving suggestions is not included.

Note: This book is for informational purposes and is not intended to provide medical advice. Neither Publications International, Ltd., nor the authors, editors or publisher takes responsibility for any possible consequences from any treatment, procedure, exercise, dietary modification, action, or applications of medication or preparation by any person reading or following the information in this cookbook. The publication of this book does not constitute the practice of medicine, and this cookbook does not replace your physician, pharmacist or health-care specialist. **Before undertaking any course of treatment or nutritional plan, the authors, editors and publisher advise the reader to check with a physician or other health-care provider.**

Not all recipes in this cookbook are appropriate for all people with diabetes. Health-care providers, registered dietitians and certified diabetes educators can help design specific meal plans tailored to individual needs.

pil Publications International, Ltd.